Okanagan College LRC

OK LIBRARY
00649400 BIA

WITHDR

D0536261

K

The Soldier Off Du

Domestic Aspects of Military Life at Fort Chambly under the French Régime as Revealed by Archaeological Objects

86982

François Miville-Deschênes

Studies in Archaeology
Architecture and History

National Historic Parks and Sites
Environment Canada — Parks

OKANAGAN COLLEGE LIBRARY
BRITISH COLUMBIA

©Minister of Supply and Services Canada 1987.

Available in Canada through authorized bookstore agents and other bookstores, or by mail from the Canadian Government Publishing Centre, Supply and Services Canada, Hull, Quebec, Canada K1A 0S9.

L'original français s'intitule **Quand ils ne faisaient pas la guerre ... ou, l'aspect domestique de la vie militaire au fort Chambly pendant le régime français d'après les objets archéologiques** (n⁰ de catalogue R61-2/9-34F). En vente au Canada par l'entremise de nos agents libraires agréés et autres librairies, ou par la poste au Centre d'édition du gouvernement du Canada, Approvisionnements et Services Canada, Hull, Québec, Canada K1A 0S9.

Price Canada: $7.50
Price outside Canada: $9.00
Price subject to change without notice.

Catalogue No.: R61-2/9-34E
ISBN: 0-660-12216-2
ISSN: 0821-1027

Published under the authority
of the Minister of the Environment,
Ottawa, 1987.

Translated by the Department of the Secretary of State.
Design and cover: Louis D. Richard.
Cover photo: Jean Jolin

The opinions expressed in this report are those of the author and not necessarily those of Environment Canada.

Parks publishes the results of its research in archaeology, architecture, and history. A list of titles is available from Research Publications, Environment Canada — Parks, 1600 Liverpool Court, Ottawa, Ontario K1A 1G2.

CONTENTS

Submitted for publication 1982, by François Miville-Deschênes, Material Culture Research, Quebec Regional Office, Environment Canada — Parks, Quebec.

ACKNOWLEDGEMENTS

I wish to thank Gisèle Piédalue, the archaeologist, and Cyrille Gélinas, the historian, who made it possible for this study to appear in its present form. They provided much information and gave generously of their time to help me refine hypotheses or clarify obscure points. I must also mention my fellow researchers, specialists in fields related to mine, whose knowledge and expertise have been of such benefit to me: René Chartrand, Simon Courcy, Hélène Deslauriers, Yvon Desloges, and Olive Jones. They have greatly helped, and greatly enriched, this study.

I also wish to thank Louise Bernard, who let me go beyond the strict bounds imposed by objects unearthed by archaeology. I was thus able to broaden the scope of my research through a more comprehensive approach to material culture.

Finally, I thank Nicole Bergeron, who showed great patience during the difficult process of sorting fragments into objects and describing them.

PREFACE

The important architectural remains of Fort Chambly were almost completely excavated between 1976 and 1978. Archaeological surveillance during the restoration phase, which began in 1979, made it possible to collect and record a host of artifacts in addition to the stratigraphic and architectural data that were added to the historical information. And in a parallel movement, history revealed its secrets gradually as material in the archives was carefully examined and research reports were written.

In this work I have not attempted to bring all these elements together. Instead, on the basis of artifacts brought to light and other evidence of material culture, I have tried to portray the domestic life of Fort Chambly's inhabitants as they may have lived it during the French régime.

INTRODUCTION

The subject, though seemingly vast, is contained within certain precise limits. The testimony of artifacts found during the archaeological excavation of the site, which is what is offered here, is just one piece of a puzzle that, once assembled, will give us a more complete picture of Fort Chambly and its place in history.

Definition of the Subject

The title of this work, though as prosaic as it is long, still requires some explanation.

Domestic Aspects ...

"Domestic aspects" means non-military activities that took place at Fort Chambly. Since the fort was occupied by military men, it is true, in a sense, that all their activities were military or, more precisely, were coloured by the fact that they belonged to the army. However, to meet their human needs, the men performed such universal acts as eating, dressing, grooming, amusing themselves, etc. The specific nature of these activities will be described, leaving aside military exercises, arms drill, guard duty, and the many other activities prescribed by the army code.

... Of Military Life ...

Military men are either common soldiers or officers. The distinction is important because it implies distinct differences in social status, cultural origin, and socioeconomic background. Fort Chambly is a microsociety that, though not wholly masculine, is made for men. That fact must be remembered when interpreting military as opposed to civilian life. For example, sewing-related objects are not associated with women, as would be the case in a family dwelling of the time. And since the day-to-day life of the fort's occupants was likely monotonous, recreation assumes a special importance. In short, a community of men, living at some remove from the city and organized into a strict hierarchy, does not always behave like a group of civilians of both sexes.

... At Fort Chambly under the French Régime ...

There was not one Fort Chambly but three forts of the same name succeeding one another on the same site. The first two forts each consisted of a wooden palisade enclosing the buildings required for garrison life. The original fort, built in 1665, burned in 1702 and was immediately replaced. In 1709 the second wooden fort was taken down, and work began on a stone structure. The stone fort, which took two years to complete, had an outer enclosure comprising four curtain walls and four bastions. This was paralleled by inner walls, and the space between the two walls was subdivided into rooms by partition walls on two floors. The square interior court thus created in the middle of the fort was used as a parade ground (Fig. 1).

Domestic activities were likely affected by the configuration of these forts. The stone fort certainly offered the garrison more space and more comfort in comparison with the ruder lifestyle that must have prevailed in the two earlier forts.

... As Revealed
by Archaeological Objects

Objects bear witness to the life of mankind because they have been produced, acquired, and used by members of particular societies and cultures. By studying modes of manufacture, acquisition, and consumption, we can use objects to formulate hypotheses on the way people once lived. In trying to imagine what a culture was like, we can also look at its particular materials and techniques, and study the meaning, the function, and perhaps even the relative status that it gave to various objects.

However, objects unearthed archaeologically, which were all abandoned by their original owners, only tell part of the story, and this makes the task of interpretation more difficult. In addition to being lost, left behind, burned, thrown out, broken, or faultily made, these objects have been buried in the ground (not their intended location) and have suffered the ravages of time and corrosion. To make them speak more clearly, other sources, such as written records, are needed. But despite these problems, it is important to study artifacts that are collected and dated as a result of archaeological excavations. The major aim of research in this area is the most exact reconstruction one can make of a specific material environment.

In the case of Fort Chambly, the excavated artifacts have an even greater value because of gaps in the written historical record:

When we turn to the official archives (Colonies, Marine, War), which are well-known sources, the problem of documentation is a real one. On a subject as specific as the one that concerns us here, this type of source is disappointingly silent. Some interesting facts can, of course, be collected here and there. But when we want to go beyond military organization to consider the material, moral or spiritual conditions of life, or to follow the troops in their daily activities, especially in the forts, the available written information is so disparate and incoherent that its use is a tricky and difficult business.[1]

By comparing artifacts with archival and secondary sources, we will better understand the everyday life and material circumstances of these military men.

10

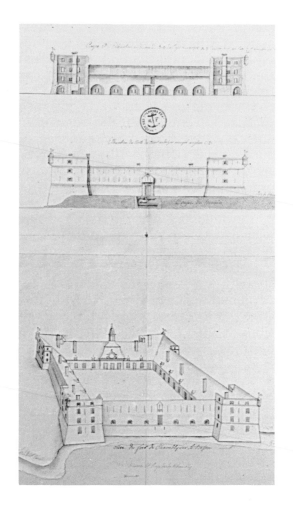

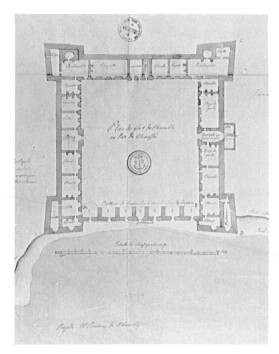

1 Plan of Fort Chambly in 1750. (France, Bibliothèque nationale; copy in the Public Archives of Canada, National Map Collection, C-20899.)

Explanation of Methodology

Artifacts, because of their peculiar nature, must be interpreted differently from other sources of information. The first part of this work looks at several aspects of Fort Chambly and locates it in its various contexts. Then, after a glance at geography, Chambly's history is described through historical information, stratigraphical data, and statistics applied to the artifacts. The task is to identify the specific characteristics of each period of occupation of the site, including the context — only a mere pinpoint in time — of the fire of 1702. Part One ends with a resumé of Chambly's social context.

The second part of the work explains the presence and use of the stone fort's artifacts. I chose this period of occupation because it is evidenced by the largest number of objects, is the most clearly delimited by stratigraphic analysis, and is historically the most representative of life in a stable garrison. Reconstruction of the site has also focussed on the stone fort. In Part Two, classes of objects are analyzed in the light of documentary data. Categories mentioned in Chambly's archives but absent from the collection are considered in this section.

The artifacts were processed as follows. Fragments were first gathered into objects, an object being defined as one or more fragments making up or representing a real, once-existing object. According to the criteria used by the Material Culture Research Group, Historical and Archaeological Research, Quebec Regional Office, Environment Canada — Parks, Quebec, an object can be complete, reconstructable, incomplete, or fragmentary. (In the following text the state of the objects described is not always indicated.) Grouping fragments together into objects, though a long and tedious process, is very important to the serious study of material culture. Indeed, the concept of the object is much more significant than that of the fragment, even if it implies a first interpretation, because it brings us much closer to the users of the original objects.

Once grouped into objects, the fragments were assigned functions according to their form. These functions were named from "Techniques, fonctions et usages des objets: répertoire des mots-clés," produced by the Material Culture Research Group. The glossary categorizes the major functions comprising the activities of the culture whose history is being studied. The main characteristics of the objects so defined were then entered on punch cards for computer processing. To better interpret variances in the proportions of materials and functions, I used statistics drawn from synthetical tables.

Since these tables were designed to take inventory of the recovered objects, they have not been reproduced here. Illustrating the representation of functions are concise graphs on which function categories are represented by the X axis and percentages by the Y axis. The left part of each graph shows the major functional categories: working of materials, acquisition, consumption, social and ideological objects, undetermined functions. The right part shows the subfunctions of consumption: food, narcotics, medication, clothing, personal care, construction. Since consumption always accounts for more than 70 per cent of objects, that category had to be broken down. The tables do not include categories for which no object was found, and one must look elsewhere to take those gaps into account.

Six tables were prepared: one for each of the three forts, one for the fire stratum, one for these four contexts together, and one for all French objects. Though I decided to select only objects from French archaeological contexts, these were sometimes contaminated by artifacts of the British period. In the later contexts I chose objects that clearly showed French origins, such as Saintonge ceramics or blue-green glass. English objects dating from the end of the 17th or from the 18th century, if found in a French context, were deemed to be artifacts used (or possibly used) by the French, and were retained in the study. The same approach was taken for the few pieces of Dutch, Italian, Spanish, and German ceramics in the collection.

The first four tables are integrated with the historical data. The dated contexts as a whole establish a general scheme, and the general table includes French objects not found in French contexts. The British occupants could not have brought these objects with them or imported them from France because the British exclusively used products from their empire or from England itself. This is so obvious that it is hard to find an author who says so explicitly. After the Conquest, Canada retained its colonial status because England wanted a new colony as another outlet for its manufactured goods.[2] I also had to consider these French objects even though they were not in their "normal" places because of stratigraphic disturbances or because they had been left behind by the French and used by the British. Some of these objects are included because they are representative of the life of the French garrison, but to eliminate as much uncertainty as possible, I dealt only with artifacts bearing marks of their origin.

One factor makes the percentages less representative. The "narcotics" subfunction includes the category of pipes, whose number has traditionally been determined at Parks by counting pipe tips only. Unfortunately, that approach gives results that are not always representative. For example, if a lot includes ten pipe fragments, none of which is a pipe tip, no object is counted, although the ten artifacts might represent two, three, or even ten separate objects. While there are obvious reasons for using this procedure, the reader must remember its drawbacks. I have, however, followed it to allow comparison of this work with tables for other sites.

THE GEOGRAPHICAL, HISTORICAL, AND SOCIAL CONTEXTS

Fort Chambly's existence is closely bound up with the importance of the Richelieu River in the history of New France. The defence of this waterway, and thus of the colony, absorbed many human and financial resources.

Geography

Since it has become commonplace to emphasize the importance of waterways in the communications system of New France, the Richelieu needs merely to be located in this network:

The axis formed by the Hudson River, Lake Champlain, and the Richelieu River, whose waters flow into Lake St-Pierre above Trois-Rivières, was certainly the most important natural route connecting New France and the English colonies. Montreal and New York were roughly located at either end of this great highway.... This interconnected network [Lake Champlain] and the Richelieu River covers a distance of 210 miles. Lake Champlain alone is more than 107 miles long and approximately 12 miles wide at its widest point. The Richelieu itself is easily navigable except for the rapids from St-Jean to Chambly. The river drops only one foot per mile from the border to St-Jean, but below St-Jean it drops more rapidly, at up to six feet per mile. From Chambly to Sorel the river is fairly calm, though because of shallows, large boats cannot navigate it in the summer and fall. In the spring, high water levels produced by floods allow easy navigation. At a very early period, people realized the importance of fortifying this much-travelled river route.[1]

Such is the importance of the Richelieu. An easily navigable waterway, it connected the British colonies to the heart of New France and offered access to the land of the Iroquois who lived on the southern shore of Lake Ontario. It was a route for both escape and invasion.

The fort dominated the river and overlooked the foot of the rapids at one end of a basin where the Richelieu's bed broadened out. Upstream from the fort, the sharp change in elevation stopped or slowed navigation and allowed closer surveillance of shipping. Downstream were calm waters where friendly vessels of all sizes could tie up.

Table 1

Functions of Objects from Fort Chambly under the French Régime (Per Cent)

Functions	1st Wooden Fort	Fire Stratum	2nd Wooden Fort	Stone Fort	French Régime	General
Work on materials	12.08	14.43	3.80	7.63	9.94	7.84
Acquisition	2.42	3.48	1.90	1.32	2.22	1.93
Consumption						
Food	43.96	48.26	65.71	59.80	53.68	52.41
Narcotics	11.11	10.95	9.52	11.96	11.18	8.58
Medication	0	0	0	1.33	0.49	0.37
Clothing	3.39	6.47	1.90	2.00	3.43	2.77
Personal care	0.48	1.00	0.95	1.33	0.98	0.74
Construction	0	0	0	0.33	0.12	0.09
Undetermined	15.40	7.96	14.29	10.30	11.55	20.20
Total	74.40	74.64	92.37	87.05	81.43	85.16
Social and ideo- logical objects	3.86	1.50	0	0.66	1.59	1.29
Undetermined	7.25	5.97	1.90	3.32	4.79	3.78

The Site: Historical Summary of the Forts
and Overview of the Artifacts

The First Wooden Fort
(1665-1702)

Historical Summary

When the first fort was built in 1665, Louis XIV was setting the historical scene. He had just assumed control of his empire and wanted to establish himself as an absolute monarch. The pursuit of his objective led to a series of measures and undertakings that were to typify the man and his reign. Strict policies defined the status of colonies, deemed to be providers of raw materials to the mother country and receivers of manufactured goods in return. To ensure the success of this trade, the colonies had to have institutions and regulations, and above all, be at peace. This could not be said of New France, where the Iroquois constantly threatened the fur trade — and the lives of the colonists. To ensure more settled times, troops and fortifications were proposed. The king's new policy produced the Carignan-Salières regiment and the forts along the Richelieu, of which Chambly was one.[2]

First constructed as a base for expeditions to subdue the Iroquois, Fort Chambly became a depot and staging point in a rather defensive strategy. When the Iroquois renewed hostilities in 1684, relying on their speed, agility, and ability to disappear into the wilderness, Chambly could only serve as a fortress or defensive establishment. At that time, since it had a small garrison, the fort provided asylum for the local civilians. From 1689 on, when the colonial British became the enemy, the fort continued to play its defensive role, since New France had to think of defending its own territory rather than invading that of the enemy.

The Artifacts

The graph in Table 2, presenting functions of artifacts from the first wooden fort, shows certain general trends found in all tables (see Table 1). The most important item is consumption (74.4 %). It is followed by working of materials (12.08 %), undetermined functions (7.25 %), social and ideological objects (3.86 %), and acquisition (2.42 %).

In Table 2's breakdown of consumption, it is food that predominates (43.96 %), followed by narcotics (11.11 %), clothing (3.39 %), and personal care (0.48 %). Medication and construction are not represented.

These percentages reveal a predominance of consumption, especially because of the food function. Transportation and communications, as elsewhere on the site, are absent. Other functions and subfunctions are not well represented, and except for work on materials, do not even reach ten per cent. Coarse earthenware, tin-glazed earthenware, and iron account for more than half of all materials found. In the category of work on materials, objects used for working cloth have a significant value of 8.21 per cent. Acquisition is represented only by side arms.

These figures do not reflect what

Table 2

Functions of Objects: First Wooden Fort and Fire Stratum

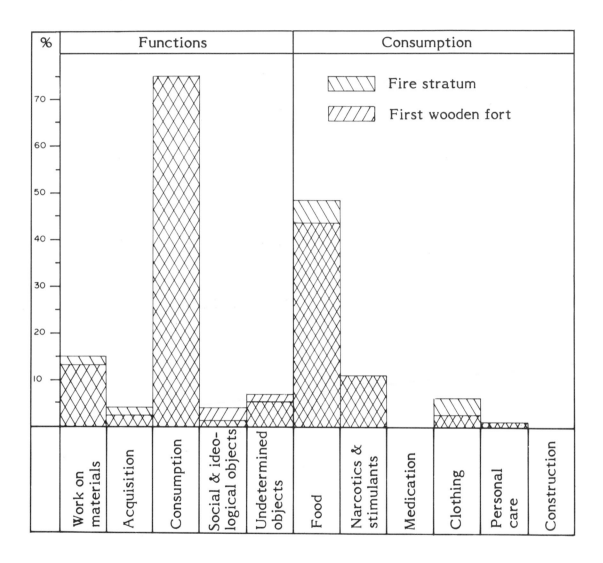

historical research tells us about officers' possessions in the 17th century:

> Officers could transport personal effects on the king's ships free of charge. They brought many fine furnishings to Montreal, like the ebony cabinet, chests covered in Moroccan leather, armchairs decorated with strips of Hungarian needlepoint, Caribbean rug, and high-warp tapestry pieces worth 400 *livres* that decorate the room. Officers' effects also included cushioned chairs,

tapestry-covered tables, feather beds even for children, sheets, various utensils, gilt-framed mirrors, all kinds of knickknacks, porcelain, and silverware. All the officers had silver items such as plates, candlesticks, etc., which would on occasion be wagered....[3]

If these luxury items crossed the ocean, porcelain, silver utensils, candlesticks, and crystal may well have come to Fort Chambly in the baggage of some well-to-do officer. However, 1665-1702 is an era of pioneers, and the inhabitants of this isolated fort likely made do with a few pieces of tin-glazed earthenware and some ordinary glass tumblers.

The Fire of 1702

Historical Summary

The first fort burned down in the winter of 1702. Damage was so great that another fort was constructed to replace it. The builders followed another plan, but used the wood and hardware that could be recovered from the ruins. The recovery very process was still incomplete on 24 July 1702.[4] It would seem that the ashes were carefully sifted for any usable material, then spread evenly over the site with rakes and shovels. The ash may have been covered with a layer of earth, but probably was not.[5] Then the new fort was built; construction was in progress in November 1702.[6]

The Artifacts

From an archaeological point of view, it would have been interesting to associate one or the other of the wooden forts with the fire stratum, which was identified during the excavations by its position in relation to other strata and by its very black colour. However, the fire is an event too limited in time (one night in the winter of 1702) to be compared with periods of occupation that extended over several years.

Logically, the fire-stratum artifacts should come from the first fort. However, the stratum is very shallow, very disturbed by reconstruction, and probably located at the level occupied by the second fort's inhabitants. Consequently, it must contain objects from the second fort. Confusion is also reflected in the stratification, so that one cannot attribute artifacts from the fire layer to one period or the other with any degree of certainty.[7]

In a search for other clues, I took another tack. Using the graphs as models representing functions, I superimposed the fire-stratum graph on the graphs of the first and second forts, to see which one gave the closest fit (see Tables 2 and 3).

The first and second forts have similar models. Columns rise and fall together, though the percentage of objects per function is not exactly the same. For example, consumption is much higher in the second fort than in the first, while the categories of social and ideological objects and working of materials are lower. Acquisition is about the same in both cases. Fire-stratum values are closer to those of the first fort, which seems to suggest that the fire layer's objects belong to the first fort. The breakdown of consumption in the second part of the graphs shows the same pattern: both the first fort and the

Table 3

Functions of Objects: Second Wooden Fort and Fire Stratum

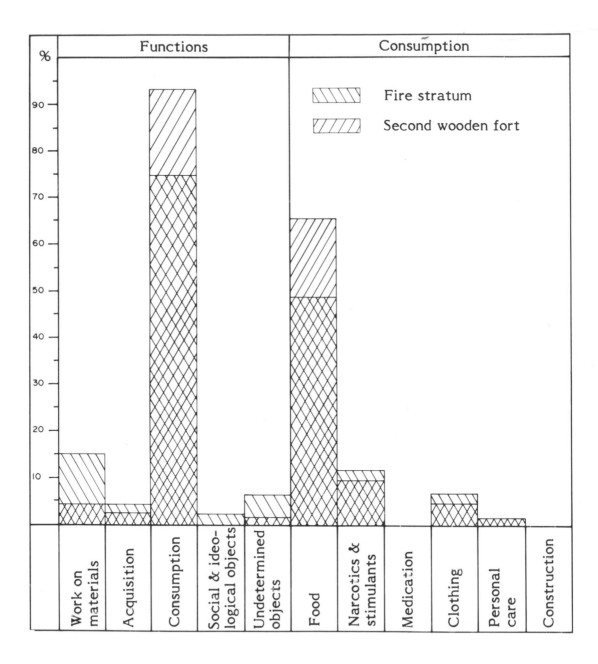

fire stratum have high percentages in the categories of narcotics and clothing. Since this correspondence is not conclusive, ceramics were also compared visually in an effort to establish closer connections between the artifacts of the fire stratum and those of the first fort.

However, in comparing the tin-glazed earthenware found in the fire stratum and in the two forts, we arrived at just the opposite of the conclusion drawn from the functional graphs. In fact, the first fort mostly had common ceramics covered with unadorned white enamel. The few exceptions to this rule include three pieces whose only decoration is a simple blue band. Some brown tin-glazed earthenware was found as well. The attribution of ceramics to various periods is based on a stratigraphic division done after the excavations. In that division, lots containing brown tin-glazed earthenware were attributed to the first wooden fort (1665-1702) on account of their position. However, documentary research has shown that brown tin-glazed earthenware was not invented until 1707 and did not reach New France until about 1720.[8] This shows that the occupation level of the first fort was also disturbed, which adds to the confusion. The ceramics of the fire stratum and of the second fort have more in common. In both cases we find many decorated pieces and a total absence of brown tin-glazed earthenware. In the case of coarse earthenware, a higher proportion of objects of local or foreign manufacture is found in the fire stratum and in the second fort, while the first fort is almost exclusively represented by pieces of French origin.

These few characteristics, though general in nature, are sufficient evidence of the confusion in the fire stratum. With the consent of the archaeologist responsible for excavating the site, I therefore decided not to include objects from this problem context in the study of either wooden fort. This approach will, I trust, reduce the margin of error in calculating percentages for the three structures.

The Second Wooden Fort (1702-1709)

Historical Summary

Little is known about the structure built in 1702. It also had a palisade, and it included two buildings constructed on stone foundations: a powder magazine and another structure with a cellar, which was used both as a store and as a main building.[9] The historical context of the second wooden fort need not be emphasized, as the destruction of the first fort by fire is an event unrelated to social and political circumstances. The fort was replaced; a fort at Chambly was still considered essential.

The Artifacts

The representation of object functions for this period is generally much the same as for the first fort; however, there are some differences. Consumption is much more important, accounting for 92.37 per cent of the objects (Tables 1 and 3). This obviously corresponds to a decline in the other categories. For example, working of materials (3.80 %) is only a third of what it was in the first fort. The same is true for undetermined objects (1.90 %). Objects reflecting social and ideological patterns are reduced to zero, while acquisition stays at the same level (1.90 %). Here again, acquisition is represented only by side arms, and working of materials by work on cloth. In both cases a smaller number of objects is involved. In the area of materials used, there is more tin-glazed earthenware (36.19 %), less iron (6.67 %), and the same amount of coarse earthenware (32.38 %). In the breakdown of consumption, there is a slight increase in the food function, which is still the leader (65.71 %), and a decline in narcotics-related objects (9.52 %).

The Stone Fort
(1709-1760)

Historical Summary

By the time the stone enclosure replaced the palisade, Chambly's historical context had changed. France was involved in an international conflict (the War of the Spanish Succession, 1702-13) and was once again England's adversary. New France had asked the king for subsidies to improve or repair its fortifications. However, the king was preoccupied by conflict in the European arena and turned a deaf ear to these requests. Meanwhile, in the fall of 1709, the British colonists assembled large forces to the south of Lake Champlain. The threat was so serious that Governor Vaudreuil and Intendant Raudot took it upon themselves to order the construction of the stone fort. When the minister of the Marine was informed, all he could do was grant permission to complete what had already been started.[10] Chambly's inhabitants now faced cannonballs rather than arrows, and stone walls offered more resistance. However, the Treaty of Utrecht was soon signed (1713) and hostilities ceased. Attention now focussed on catching smugglers, who regularly went up the Richelieu on their way to Albany, where their furs fetched higher prices. Fort Chambly was supposed to stop the illicit traffic. In the 1730s the forts of St-Frédéric and St-Jean were built farther up the Richelieu. These forts were better placed to monitor the British and, if necessary, stop them. Chambly thus lost its strategic importance, but continued to serve as a staging point and depot to provision the other two forts.[11] However, during the final French war in Canada, Chambly regained its former prestige:

At the outbreak of the last war to be fought under the French régime, Chambly found itself at the very heart of the conflict. Despite the weakness of its walls, it helped to speed up communications among the various forts along the Richelieu, and it was a place to store material, to bivouac, and to assemble troops. All traffic between Montreal or Quebec and the forts of the Richelieu passed by Chambly, which thus became a significant factor despite its defensive weakness.[12]

The Artifacts

The objects of the period of the stone fort are distributed in somewhat the same way as those of the second wooden fort (Tables 1 and 4). Function values as a percentage of total objects are: working of materials, 7.63 per cent; acquisition, 1.32 per cent; consumption, 87.05 per cent; social and ideological objects, 0.66 per cent; and undetermined objects, 3.32 per cent. Working of materials is still best represented by work on cloth (6.64 %). On the other hand, acquisition now includes two elements of equal value, fishing and side arms (0.66 %). In the breakdown of consumption, food accounts for 59.80 per cent of objects, narcotics have a value of 11.96 per cent, and medication is finally present at 1.33 per cent. Clothing remains at 2.0 per cent, as in the second wooden fort, personal care increases to 1.33 per cent, and construction is present for the first time at 0.33 per cent.

In the area of materials used, a striking increase appears in refined white stoneware (9.97 %) and fine porcelain (7.31 %). Coarse and tin-glazed earthenware decline as a result, but are still quite well represented (20.27 % and 23.59 % respectively). Clear lead glass (crystal) substantially increases to 3.65 per cent in the stone fort, as compared to 0.48 per cent for the first wooden fort and zero for the second. Furthermore, representation of dark green glass now reaches ten per cent.

When attempts to interpret this information led to historical sources, one realizes that the average soldier took very few possessions with him. These usually consisted of his uniform, civilian clothing, weapons, and some personal effects. Appendix A reproduces a list of the goods belonging to a soldier of the Chambly garrison, Sergeant Bonin *dit* Laforest; however, the reader should remember that the man was arrested for theft.

Soldiers' incomes were modest; they had to travel light, and in their postings the state supplied them with furniture, bedding, and some utensils. It is thus reasonable to suppose that their possessions were few. Those who were able to make a little money by selling drink, clothing, or fish, or by hiring out their services,[13] probably either held onto their nest eggs or spent their money on more ephemeral pleasures. The assets of Bonin *dit* Laforest mainly consisted of notes of exchange.

Soldiers were certainly not all in the position of Yves Bouillette *dit* Laviolette, for whom the following plea was written after the Conquest:

> Finally [Bouillette] found himself at the siege of Fort Chambly, where he lost the ownership of a piece of land he had cleared with the permission of His Majesty, because he had married a girl of said Fort Chambly. This piece of land was destroyed by the English.... When the English took said Fort Chambly, the aforementioned Bouillette was made a prisoner of war with the rest of the garrison, and lost all his possessions.[14]

Appendix B offers an example of officers' possessions in that period:

Table 4

Functions of Objects: Stone Fort

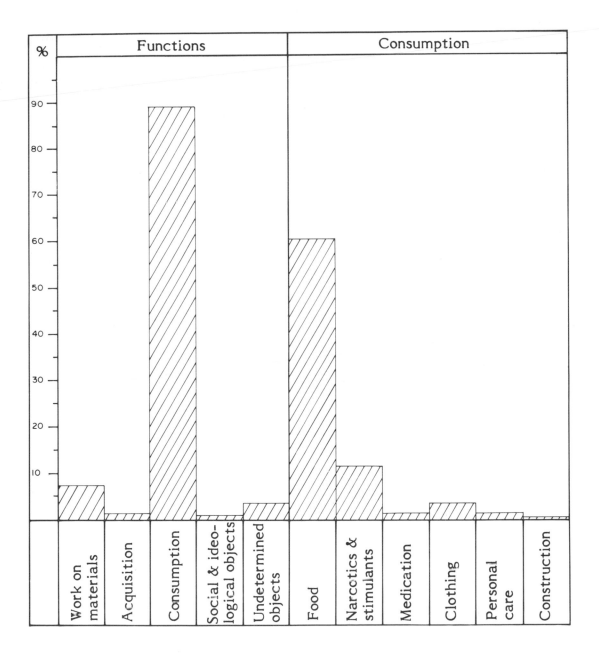

an extract from the inventory of goods that Lieutenant Joseph Déjourdy de Cabanac had in Montreal in 1737, probably in a secondary dwelling. Clothing has been omitted from this list.

Overview of the Artifacts as a Whole

The collection of artifacts from the Chambly site comprises 207 objects from the first wooden fort, 105 from the second, 303 from the stone fort, 201 from the fire stratum, and 270 out of context. There are thus 1086 objects in all, of which 816 are from dated contexts. It is unfortunate that so few objects were found because one cannot be sure that they are representative. Percentages are more reliable when applied to large quantities and are thus more representative for the stone fort than for the two wooden ones.

Comparing the graphs of the three forts reveals a break between the first wooden fort and the second, whose values are closer to those of the stone fort. This discontinuity is particularly noticeable in the categories of working of materials, consumption (mainly because of food), and social and ideological objects.

According to historian Jacques Mathieu,[15] New France was swept by great socioeconomic changes in the early 18th century. The population grew rapidly. Beaver exports declined, though trade in general was on the upswing. The economy became more diversified, and more and more people took up farming:

The philosophers, like some ministers, had taken to saying that New France, and the colonies in general, cost much and brought in little. The government's statement of income and expenditures seemed to support this view, since the colonial undertaking recorded a deficit on the public accounts. However, this estimate, which ignored economic side-effects, did not consider New France's contribution to the wealth of the mother country. The trade in furs, agricultural produce, and manufactured objects made men rich, but their profits did not appear on the official balance sheet. Through resource development and colonial market expansion, New France had become a highly profitable concern. The chambers of commerce that opposed its transfer after Montcalm's defeat on the Plains of Abraham were not mistaken.[16]

Many people now worked the land, and during the 18th century, city dwellers and "habitants" developed distinctly different lifestyles. The cities contained the social class of people who had more money and education, and who sought refinement.

Houses were mostly made of stone. They contained paintings, drawings and tapestries, and sometimes musical instruments and rich furnishings as well. City dwellers spent all they could on canopied beds, carved pine wardrobes, fine bedding, silver cutlery, and porcelain dishes. They often dressed elegantly, in clothes made from imported French fabrics.[17]

From the beginning of the 18th century, New France moved at a faster pace and became more prosperous and dynamic. This trend is particularly noticeable during the peace that followed the Treaty of Utrecht in 1713. It is both plausible and probable that the different distributions of object functions for the 1665-1702 and 1702-1760 periods reflect the new situation.

The stone fort has a greater diversity of materials and more luxurious ceramics and glassware. These correspond exactly to the period of peace. (The problem of the stone fort's British ceramics and glassware will be considered in Part Two). The officers who brought these objects were mostly city dwellers, and the existence of a stone fort likely encouraged them (and some common soldiers as well) to create a more comfortable environment. The new structure offered more space, comfort and security, and had rather few occupants into the bargain.

Table 5 gives the percentage representation of various functions for all dated contexts of the French period. Table 1 shows that these values fall more or less midway between the values for the first fort and the mean of the percentages for the two later forts. The usefulness of Table 1, which presents data on all French contexts, is thus limited by the significant break in 1702. Table 6, which has figures for all French objects, including those found out of context, is more helpful. It shows that the percentage representation of consumption has risen. This is to be expected, since the objects out of context are made of ceramic and glass, which are most commonly used in this function. The increase, which amounts to four per cent, is not reflected in the breakdown of consumption because most of the out-of-context artifacts could not be attributed to specific subfunctions. All that can be said is that these items were used for consumption.

Few objects from the French periods were unearthed at Chambly. This fact can be explained in various ways. Since Chambly was a campaign fort, had few occupants, and was not in a town, consumer goods were likely used to a limited extent. Furthermore, when the first fort was built by pioneering soldiers in 1665, the surrounding area had few inhabitants and the colony was still being organized. Few objects were found from the second fort because it was taken down after only seven years of occupation. Objects from this fort were probably set aside, to be re-used in the new stone structure. The stone fort was certainly more comfortable, and its occupants, especially the officers, were perhaps prompted to surround themselves with more valuable, and more numerous, objects. However, when New France surrendered, officers and men likely took their personal effects with them, and the objects left behind may have been re-used by the British.

A final point concerning the archaeological remains of Fort Chambly is important. It was built on the banks of the Richelieu, which was no doubt used as a dump, and its latrines emptied into the river. Most objects recovered by archaeol-

Table 5

Functions of Objects: All French Contexts

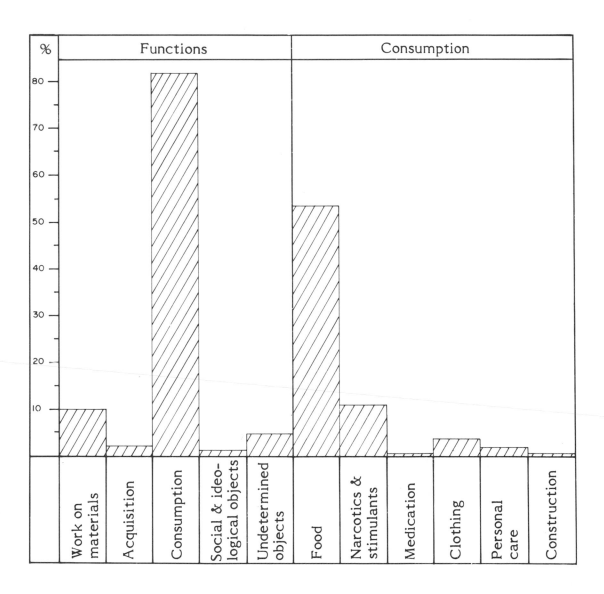

ogy are cast-offs that have been buried through the action of nature, as a result of land redevelopment, or because they were lost, thrown away, or trodden under foot, but at Fort Chambly the Richelieu likely swallowed up most objects of this kind. Since the site also went through many changes, it is not surprising that so many remains have disappeared.

In order to summarize what the

Table 6

Functions of Objects: All French Objects

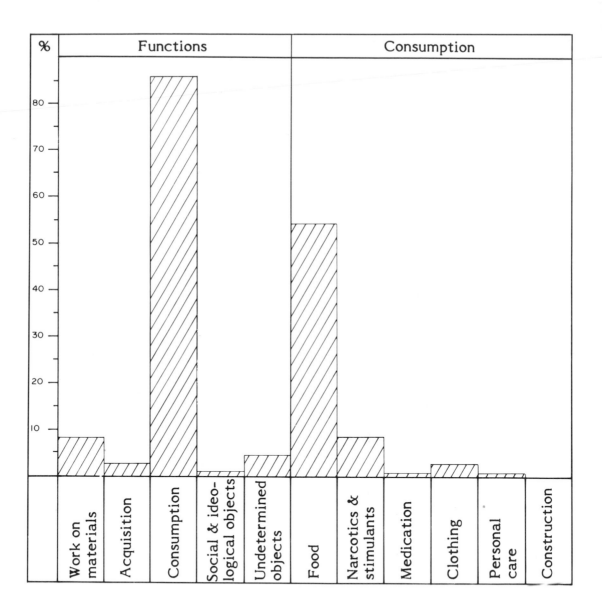

excavations brought to light, the representation of functions have been analyzed in a descriptive way. This approach does, however, give us some clues by stressing the difference between the objects of the first and second wooden forts and by showing the greater affinity between the second wooden fort and the stone fort.

Table 7

Garrison Forces

Year	Number	Year	Number
1667	100 men, of whom 30 were sent to Fort Ste. Anne*	1741	30 men and 5 officers*
		1742	6 men, 1 officer and 1 sergeant*
1668	At least 66 men**		
		1746	5 men, 1 officer and 1 sergeant*
1671	70 men***		
1679	0***	1747	25 men***
1681	0*	1751	41 soldiers, 1 captain, 1 lieutenant, 2 ensigns, 2 cadets, 2 sergeants, 3 corporals and 2 drummers*
1686	18 men, 1 lieutenant and 2 sergeants*		
1687-1699	Generally 50 men (1 company)***		
		1754	15 men and 1 captain*
1691	In August, 200 men**	1757	80 men**
1699-1741	Generally 20 to 25 men*	1759	20 men**
1704	23 men*	1760	150 men, including civilian employees**
1708	16 men*		
		1760	On capitulation, 71 men were made prisoners**
1711	Approximately 100 men*		
1720	Approximately 50 men*		

```
*     Gélinas 1981: personal conversation
**    Nadon 1965: 5-21
***   Gélinas 1977: 121-23
```

OKANAGAN COLLEGE LIBRARY
BRITISH COLUMBIA

The importance of consumption at Chambly is not surprising. Consumption is important on all sites. Since most building hardware was also excluded, the high representation of consumption at Chambly is mostly due to the food function. This function commonly outweighs all others, at least in part because of the nature of the artifacts. Food, clothing, and shelter are the three great human needs, and in this study I intentionally ignored shelter-related objects except for a few that improved the comfort of the building. And since buried cloth rots, few clothing-related items remain. The food function thus predominates in the tables because most food-related objects are glass or ceramic and are well preserved in the ground.

The Social Environment

Troop Strength

In 1712 Governor Vaudreuil noted that the stone fort could accommodate a regular garrison of 500 soldiers and 500 more in an emergency.[18] However, the fort was seldom occupied to that extent (see Table 7). Except during its first and last years, the stone fort had a small garrison. However, the historical sources from which these figures are drawn refer to specific moments and do not necessarily give a true historical picture. In any case, Table 7 seems to suggest that Chambly usually had between 25 and 100 men (their actual number being closer to 25 than 100) except for a short period (1742-47) when the authorities reduced the garrison to five or six soldiers and their officer.[19] Even 100 soldiers is only a fifth of the stone fort's capacity. The men of Chambly must have had more room than their counterparts elsewhere.

The last years of the French occupation are more difficult to evaluate.

For the last years of the régime, we do not have enough information to determine the size of the garrison. It must have varied considerably. Chambly was an important bivouacking and provisioning centre. Everyday life, enlivened by the troops' comings and goings, had a special quality that broke the typical monotony of life in a remote garrison. When new army regiments arrived in New France in 1755, some of them used Chambly as winter quarters.[20] These were the Languedoc, Royal Roussillon, Guyenne, and La Reine regiments. However, not all the soldiers lived in the fort. Several were quartered in the village or on farms.[21]

These troop movements only occurred during Chambly's last years. In 1709, 1600 men encamped under its walls, and in 1711 several hundred soldiers were dispatched from the fort to counter the British threat. Other people were constantly coming and going: provision-

OKANAGAN COLLEGE LIBRARY
BRITISH COLUMBIA

ing convoys and troops on their way to Lake Champlain, Indians going down to Albany, skilled workers summoned to the fort, etc.[22]

We do not know to what degree these more or less sporadic activities are reflected in the material remains of the fort and its surroundings. Obviously, 1600 soldiers did not leave without a trace. But many questions — to what extent are these troops represented in the collection of artifacts? Can they be differentiated from the garrison troops? — must remain unanswered.

Civilian Employees

Civilian employees worked at Chambly in the service of the army, but they may not all have lived at the fort. For example, chaplains were at Chambly from 1665 to 1667 and again from 1691 to 1742. They served both the garrison and the civilian population[23] because Chambly did not have a church until 1739.

The fort appears to have had a storekeeper at all times. He performed the essential task of administering the king's store (receiving and distributing goods, preparing inventories, etc.). A baker was also hired, at least from 1699 on.[24] We know that the storekeeper and the baker worked at the fort, but not that they lived there. The marriage contract between Michelle Leber and Pierre Pépin dit Laforce,[25] king's storekeeper residing at Chambly, proves that he had his own residence. However, this was not the case in 1751 and in 1752.[26]

The position of storekeeper seems to have been coveted by several prominent men of the region, among them Antoine Grisé dit Villefranche, who was born at Chambly in 1728. In 1756 he was king's notary in the seigneuries of Chambly and de Rouville, and also storekeeper at the fort.[27] Grisé more than likely had a house at Chambly and did not have to live in the fort.

The evidence permits no conclusions as to where the storekeeper lived except that individual circumstances varied. We know even less about the baker's place of residence.

Finally, there was "a crowd of day labourers or skilled workers such as blacksmiths, locksmiths, masons, carters, and laundry women, who were hired to perform specific repair, construction or maintenance tasks."[28] Historical documents show, for example, that the blacksmith and locksmith, Jean Fort dit Laforest, went to Fort Chambly 45 times in 1730 and 1731 to repair or install hardware, and that in 1733 he performed 36 jobs of the same kind with the help of Jean-Baptiste Fleur D'Épée. During those years the blacksmith was called to the fort two or three times a month on the average.[29]

Many civilians thus had access to the fort on a daily basis. They came when called for, to attend religious services, or to meet the chaplain. These more or less regular visits may have left traces, no doubt in the form of personal effects rather than, say, ceramic ware. Such close contacts with the civilian population presumably led to some exchange of material goods.

In 1719 three soldiers of the Chambly garrison were put on trial

31

for murder. The documents of the trial provide some insight into the nature of the relations between soldiers and civilians at that time.[30] In particular:

- Three soldiers were working M. de Ramezay's sawmill.
- It seems that Sansquartier, one of the accused, though a common soldier, lived not at the fort, but in the home of a Chambly widow.
- On Candlemas, both soldiers and civilians attended Mass at the fort.
- On the eve of his death the victim, a black civilian, dined with a Chambly couple. Soldiers of the garrison were also present at the dinner.
- After dinner the victim visited the chaplain of the fort.
- The wounded victim was taken to Fort Chambly, where he died. The surgeon apparently did not treat the victim.

Portrait of the Common Soldier

Like the masses in general, the common soldiers of New France have left few traces on the historical record. Their existence can only be sketched.

In 1723 a king's order stipulated that men of the *Compagnies franches* had to be at least five *pieds* one *pouce* tall (five feet five inches in the British system of measurement, or 1.60 metres) and at least 16 years of age. Statistics on 24 garrison soldiers at Quebec from 1730 to 1760 and on 1018 soldiers at Louisbourg in 1752 show that the law was quite closely observed, since the average height of these men was indeed five *pieds* one *pouce*. Still, some of them did not meet the prescribed standard. Moreover, analysis of the ages of 164 recruits from 1748 to 1751 shows that only four had not yet turned 16.[31] Of this same group, 43 per cent were between 16 and 20, 42 per cent between 21 and 30, and about 13 per cent over 30.[32] These soldiers were very young; today, half of them would be called teenagers. This modern consideration apart, the soldiers' ages give some clues as to the climate that must have reigned in garrisons where a number of young, and even very young, men lived together. We don't have to be experts in psychology to imagine the mischief, pranks, squabbles, and laughter that must have been the norm at Chambly. And the fort was likely no stranger to profound boredom — and high ambition.

The soldiers of Canada may seem younger than those of Louisbourg because of the smaller number of individuals observed in Canada. However, I think that the troops of Canada were younger because the Louisbourg authorities insisted on recruiting soldiers who had trades, and were thus somewhat older. Official correspondence, at least, suggests that the authorities in Canada were less concerned about this.[33]

These young men were forced to lead a rather nomadic existence. Approximately every two years garrisons were exchanged among the various posts, apparently to prevent the troops from getting into a rut and to give them a chance to acquire varied experience. The policy was not without its problems.

The officers, who often had families and one or more properties in the various administrative districts, were sometimes reluctant to move with their companies, or simply refused to do so. The instability of command and the multiplicity of postings must have affected discipline among the troops.[34]

Why soldiers enlisted is hard to assess and authors are divided on this complex issue. Some take a positive view:

Solicitation is often cited as a means of recruiting individuals who, surprised in a drunken state, were induced to sign up. But in many instances, may we not be dealing with excuses advanced by soldiers who had deserted or committed other crimes and wished to reduce their punishment? Many individuals would have been sufficiently motivated to enlist by the soldiering tradition of France's frontier and coastal regions, and by the desire to improve their material circumstances and escape from poverty.[35]

And some are negative:

Recruited in haste shortly before their departure, they set sail for Canada, not knowing what awaited them because they weren't told where they were going.... They were often induced, by force or solicitation, to go off to fight far from their homeland, and far from family and friends whom they would likely never see again, for reasons that they understood poorly or not at all. This adventure must have weighed heavily upon them, enured though they were to suffering.[36]

Finally, should we believe the naturalist Pehr Kalm as historian W.J. Eccles quoted him: "[the soldiers] were very well fed and clothed, paid regularly, enjoyed good relations with their officers, and were particularly well treated on discharge"?[37]

The Officers

Historical sources show that Chambly's complement of officers usually included a commander (captain of a company), a lieutenant who assisted him and replaced him if necessary, and an ensign (see Table 7). Sometimes, but not always, there was also a sergeant. This non-commissioned officer, who had been promoted from the ranks, acted as a liaison between officers and men;[38] however, in terms of status and pay, the sergeant was more an enlisted man than he was an officer.

Officers lived at the fort during their tours of duty. It seems, however, that the commander frequently left the fort to stay at his residence or temporary lodgings. Like the commander, other officers had permanent residences or temporary lodgings, but they apparently did not have enough free time to leave the fort frequently.[39]

Cameron Nish claimed that during the second quarter of the 18th century, commanders' positions were much sought after. However, Nish referred to positions in the west, where the fur trade was a very lucrative business.[40] Since the forts of Chambly and St-Frédéric do not fall into that category, Nish deliberately omitted them.[41] He did, however, note that commanders were appointed from the rather small group of *Compagnies franches* officers.[42] Since postings changed frequently,[43] it is thus reasonable to assume that Fort Chambly's commanders were in charge of a fur-trading post at one time or another. Nish's remarks would then apply to them as well:

> The post commanders were a privileged group. They were associated with one another, or with the administrators and merchants of the colony, by ties of marriage.... It has also been established that the members of this group — again ignoring the class designation — could not be considered solely as a military élite. They were, at the very least, seigneurs, often merchants and traders, and sometimes administrators as well. Another argument refers to how the fur trade was financed and what profits it could generate. We have seen that extremely close and complex relationships existed between the so-called merchants' and military groups. These relationships were based partly on power and privilege, partly on marriage ties, and partly on capital resources. We have also seen that military men, traders and administrators all shared in the exploitation of the *Pays d'en Haut* [the interior].[44]

One way or another, the "bourgeois gentlemen of New France" must thus include Paul d'Ailleboust de Périgny, Jacques-Charles de Sabrevois, Jacques Hugues Péan de Livaudière, Antoine Pécaudy de Contrecoeur, Gaspard Adhémar de Lantagnac, Nicolas-Marie Renaud d'Avène des Méloizes, Jean-Baptiste Hertel de Rouville, and Paul-Louis de Lusignan, who were all commanders of Fort Chambly between 1716 and 1760.[45]

A portrait of the typical Chambly commander must take these facts into account. The commander was not a soldier whose sole concern was the defence of his homeland, but rather a man who had various economic interests and who played an important role in the society of New France. After all, he belonged to an élite that, in the final analysis, ran the colony. The same applied, but to a lesser degree, to his officers, for they belonged, or aspired to belong, to this élite.

Women at the Fort

Less is known about women at Fort Chambly than about any other aspect of its social life. However, some facts are known. In 1751, for example, military engineer Louis Franquet noted in the report of his voyage: "Spent the whole day with the ladies and paid a visit to Madame de Beaulac, an officer's widow who has been given a place to live in the fort."[46] Madame de Beaulac was the widow of a former commander of the fort. The other ladies were probably officers' wives.

Notarized documents pertaining to Chambly include three marriage contracts of soldiers who were garrisoned at the fort. These are dated 11 June 1690, 26 October 1741, and 5 January 1758. The first contract stipulated that the couple could live for six months with the bride's parents. Since she had received land as a dowry, by the time the six months were up, the newlyweds would presumably have built a house on the property. Detailed information of this kind is not contained in the other two contracts. Since in 1741 the garrison included only 50 men, the couple whose marriage contract was drawn up in that year may have resided in the fort. The same arrangement is plausible for the contract of 1758.[47]

However, the authorities did not encourage the presence of wives or children at the fort. In 1691, for example, Intendant Champigny complained of the abuses of Commander Blaise des Bergères in that respect: "Moreover, he there consumes a considerable quantity of foodstuffs, munitions and utensils from the store, having with him his family."[48] In 1725 Montreal Governor Longueuil and Intendant Bégon wrote to the minister of Marine that too many fires were being maintained at Chambly. To solve the problem, they suggested that the two married officers be replaced by two bachelors who would share the same room and use only one fire. A year later Governor Beauharnois implemented their proposal and was congratulated by the minister.[49] The question of women and children at Chambly is far from being settled: they were there at certain times, but perhaps only on temporary bases.

It is difficult to draw conclusions about the occupants of Fort Chambly. Their number varied considerably over the years, and little can be positively stated even about those who actually lived in the fort, in the sense that they slept and took their meals there on a day-to-day basis. Information is equally scanty regarding the relations between soldiers and officers, and between the soldiers and the habitants of the seigneury. Finally, though the presence of women at Chambly is attested, nothing definite can be said about the length of time they spent there.

Everyday life in the third fort at Chambly was probably easier and more comfortable than it had been in the two wooden forts. The new stone structure had two floors, and cellars and attics as well. It thus offered more space and better protection against the elements. The trend towards greater refinement, which appeared at the beginning of the 18th century, became more pronounced as time went on.

Archaeological objects from this period are more diverse in terms of functions and materials. There are also more objects of British origin. The list of objects still reflects the life of a garrison, and despite the presence of more luxurious items, the collection as a whole remains one of simply average quality. There are many multipurpose objects and few that have very specific functions.

Chambly's situation appears to be the same as that of Michilimackinac (1715–81):

The early French inhabitants possessed few personal items which were not essential for subsistence purposes. Most of their possessions were utilitarian and functionally generalized in nature and exhibited a low level of formal variation. It has been emphasized that many trade goods were also in common use by the French occupants. This condition had changed by the end of the French period of control. At this time, an increased use of artifact categories representing specialized activities and different status positions is noted. However, the majority of the assemblage remains generalized in terms of occupations or task application, and reflects the local subsistence and trade orientation of the population.[1]

At that time, however, when mass production and consumption were uncommon, different standards were used to measure quality of life. To define the setting in which people lived and to establish the basis of a very approximate comparison, consider the description of the interior of a peasant's house in the France of Louis XV:

Peasant houses are almost all poor and unhealthy. Though they are built according to models that vary from region to region, practically all of them have mud walls, and are low and dark. The peasant's roof is thatched (tiles being a mark of prosperity). The floor is of beaten earth, without flagstones. The house essentially consists of one room, whose only relative luxury is a fireplace with a broad mantelpiece, from which are hung iron and copper utensils, and a lamp to provide light. Around the fireplace are a few stools, straw chairs, and sometimes an armchair. In the middle of the room is a table with a drawer, and benches. Against the wall a cupboard holds decorated faïence, plates, salad bowls, glasses, pewter spoons, and iron forks. The richest peasants have large sideboards. Daylight filters into the room through a narrow window covered with oiled paper or very crude glass, which lets in very little light. In some regions, such as Normandy, the house has one and sometimes two bedrooms adjacent to the kitchen. But often, both in the north and in the south, there is just the one room. Beds, which are placed in the corners, sometimes have testers and, the only apparent luxury, are embellished with woollen valances. They are covered with bed-linen and cotton quilts. When the house includes a bedroom, the lady of the house decks it out rather gaily, according to her taste. There may be some pictures on the wall and printed toile curtains on the window. Poor and rich are distinguished by the bed, a symbol of prosperity. In the rich man's house, we will find a feather bed, white woollen blankets, a quilt of printed toile, and sometimes a brocaded coverlet. The poor man makes do with a straw mattress

and a blanket. Beside the bed is a chest, often carved, which contains bedding and clothing. Wardrobes are a mark of luxury, and only the richest peasants have clocks or mirrors.[2]

On the subject of goods supplied to soldiers, a letter by Intendant Hocquart, written in 1734, gives some information on the contents of the king's store:

> [The] material for the soldiers is divided up in the storekeepers' registers of Quebec, Trois-Rivières, Montreal, Fort Frontenac ..., Fort Chambly.... This material consists of tackle and gear for canoes, foodstuffs for employees of the stores, rations and special foodstuffs for military detachments moving from one garrison to another or travelling for military service to any post, bags, ... cloth, axes, buckets, material for making small repairs to boats or in the stores, oil, candles, paper and other office supplies, some customary handouts of bread, salt, and ordinary foodstuffs for the Recollets....[3]

The objects from the period of the stone fort will help to reconstruct life as it was lived at Chambly during the first half of the 18th century.

Work

Tools

The tool category is represented by a spade and three axes, one of which could not be positively identified. The other two, however, made of forged iron and steel, are felling axes of a well-known type (Fig. 2). The eyes of such axes are more or less triangular. One wooden axe

2 Felling axe made of iron and steel. The handle is wood and its end is wrapped in a piece of cloth. (Photo by J. Jolin.)

10 CM.

3 Iron or steel spade of which a part of the wooden handle remains. (Photo by J. Jolin.)

handle is partially preserved: a piece of cloth was wound around the end of the handle inserted into the eye to ensure greater security. The spade is a narrow, straight shovel whose cutting edge is missing. It was likely used for gardening or digging small holes. What remains of its handle shows that it was a rather sturdy tool (Fig. 3). A spade is more useful for turning earth than for excavating it.

The lack of tools is surprising and we have every reason to believe

that the collection of artifacts does not reflect reality. In 1734, as noted above, the king's store must have contained axes and buckets. And in 1758, goods delivered to Fort Chambly included 1000 shovels.[4] While a large number of these shovels were no doubt forwarded to other forts, the fact remains that the shovel was an essential tool. The government bought many tools, such as axes, picks, mattocks, etc., either in France or in the colony. These are mentioned in the vouchers for income and expenditures. In 1739, for example, an order was placed with Pierre Maillou of Quebec for ten large axes and 134 medium-size axes, and in 1740 a large number of assorted tools arrived from France.[5] This equipment was used, in particular, for paramilitary work performed by the troops on behalf of the state. The soldiers of Chambly were responsible, for example, for cutting the firewood required by the fort.[6] In addition, they were occasionally paid for doing other jobs. In 1730, for example, six soldiers removed "earth" from the courtyard of the fort, in 1732 some men built a road between Fort Chambly and the Ste-Thérèse portage, and in 1736 others cleared "the land around the fort."[7] Such work certainly required picks, shovels, axes, rakes, etc. It is hard to believe that a fort such as Chambly could function without a minimum of basic tools, the kind still needed today in occupied buildings (hammers, saws, screwdrivers, etc.).

The absence of tools can be explained in two ways. In the first place, statements of repairs and maintenance at Chambly for the years 1730, 1731, and 1733[8] show that skilled workers (a carpenter and a man who was a blacksmith and locksmith) came to the fort to perform certain tasks, such as assembling stoves, putting in hinges, or removing rotten beams from the guardroom. Since the garrison was not responsible for this kind of maintenance, fewer tools were needed, as the workers brought their own. Secondly, when the fort was captured in 1760, tools (like many other items) were probably left where they were and re-used by the British.

Instruments of Work

In this category, only one activity has been positively identified: sewing. What we have are 19 pins of tinned brass, most of which have lost their tin plating (Fig. 4). Their average length is 3.15 cm. They were manufactured from lengths of brass wire that were straightened, then sharpened at one end to form a point. The head of the pin was made with another piece of wire, which was rolled in a spiral around the unpointed end and lightly crimped. It was a common practice to cover this kind of pin with a coating of tin.[9]

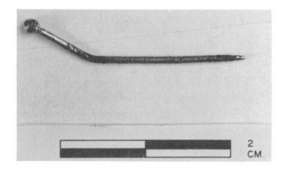

4 Tinned brass pin. (Photo by N. Royer.)

Half of a pair of scissors may also be associated with sewing. The rather small object is 13.0 cm long. The loop of the scissors has a flat cross-section, and its shank is relatively long in relation to the blade, which is thick and rounded at the

5 Shank of steel scissors. (Photo by J. Jolin.)

top (Fig. 5). The fineness of the loop suggests that this pair of scissors was used for sewing, but its short length indicates that it was used for mending rather than for making clothes. While it cannot be specifically attributed to paper cutting, which usually would require longer blades, it was not necessarily only used for sewing. Scissors would, in fact, be commonly used to cut various kinds of material, even paper if necessary.

The presence of sewing-related objects is easily explained. Soldiers who did not want to pay to have their uniforms mended had to do the work themselves; indeed, they were given thread and needles to do so.[10] Pins were used to hold cloth in place for sewing, and could also be used for mending. Pins may also have been used to hold torn cloth together, hold detached buttons in place, or replace missing buttons.

Uniforms sent to the colony came in only three sizes,[11] so it is likely that the soldiers wanted to alter them to fit better. We are all familiar with the problem of standardized small, medium, and large sizes that only seem to fit a few individuals. The problem apparently existed in the 18th century as well. Soldiers and officers, in search of comfort or elegance, no doubt adjusted their clothes to their personal measurements. Pins facilitated such alterations: shortening sleeves or legs, taking in or letting out shoulders and waist, etc.

The absence of needles is not surprising and indeed is typical of artifact collections. The most plausible explanation for this absence is that sewing, then as now, required many pins but only a few needles. Since there were fewer needles, people tried not to lose them.

Finally, some of the women of the fort must have had work baskets or sewing kits for repairing their wardrobes.

This first category, work, is characterized more by significant gaps in the record than by a great variety of tools and instruments of work. This conclusion is supported by a document of 1749, "Statement of munitions, goods and foodstuffs delivered from the king's stores at Quebec and sent to [Shedaic], on the coast of Acadia, to provide subsistence and service to the officers and men of the military, and to the inhabitants...."[12] The statement mentions 100 awls, 6 wood chisels, 1 scraper, 50 large axes, 30 medium-size axes, 6 adzes, 4 saw blades, 2 pronged hammers, 40 steel-tipped shovels, 6 mattocks, 2 ripsaws, and 2 crosscut saws.

Interior Appointments

Walls and Windows

Few traces of walls and windows remain. All we have are 116 fragments of window glass and one fragment of roughcast plaster.

Chambly's roughcast plaster remains might be very interesting were they not limited to a single fragment a few centimetres long. The fragment is rather thick (0.85 cm) and is coloured red on one side. No conclusion, of course, can be drawn on such slight evidence. The fragment was found in the inner court, in a stratum attributed to a local fire. It is thought that this fire occurred at the end of the French period though it is not mentioned in the historical record. The fire apparently damaged a part of the fort, and the debris it produced was buried in the courtyard.[13] It seems likely that at least one room was covered with roughcast. Since roughcast plaster was a luxury, the piece may have come from the commander's quarters, but this is a weak hypothesis, based as it is on one isolated fragment.

The fragments of window glass are not much more informative. Plans of the period reveal that Chambly's walls had many windows. All the fragments tell us is that these windows were covered with glass and not with oiled paper. However, the use of oiled paper, which seems to have been confined mainly to farmhouses, would have been most unusual in a fort.[14]

Of the 116 fragments of window glass, 112 have green tints and only four have blue tints. To date, no one has succeeded in showing that the use of one tint rather than the other has any particular significance.[15] Perhaps a change of manufacturer is involved. In the 18th century two methods were commonly used to manufacture window glass. In the so-called crown method, a disk-shaped piece of glass was produced by centrifugal force generated by a spinning rod. To make broad glass, a cylinder was first blown, then split and flattened. Both methods seem to have produced equally strong glass. Whatever the method used to produce Fort Chambly's window glass, the fragments seem to be thick enough to ensure adequate strength.

The tint of the window glass produced blue-green reflections in daylight. This was a common drawback at that time; clear glass only came into use much later.

In the strata dating from the British period were what seems to be two fragments of lead strips. This material was certainly used to secure windowpanes during the French régime.

Heating

Since none of the archaeological objects provide evidence for heating, we have to turn to the historical records. For example, between 1730 and 1745, people generally paid between 500 and 600 *livres* annually for 400 cords of wood.[16]

More specific information is found in the letter that Longueuil and Bégon wrote to the minister in 1725.[17] They complained that the 11 fires maintained at Fort Chambly were too many. They also listed the fires: one for the chaplain, two for the lieutenant, three for the commander, two for the guardroom, and one for each of the ensigns. Since the list mentions ten fires and since the men had a right to one fireplace per sleeping room,[18] the garrison troops (approximately 25 soldiers) must have had to make do with the single fire not specified in the letter. However, this fire could have heated two barrack rooms if it was made in a hearth open both front and back. The disparity between the comfort levels of the officers and the men is not hard to miss.

The list also reveals something about the distribution of space. The commander enjoyed the use of a kitchen, an office, and a bedroom,[19] and the other officers do not appear to have lacked for comfort either. For example, two of Chambly's ensigns had brought their wives with them and were replaced by bachelors who shared one bedroom. Much less space was provided for the common soldiers, even though so few people usually lived in the fort.

The fires that Longueuil and Bégon mentioned were made in stoves or on hearths. There was a stove in the guardroom in 1719.[20] Chambly's statements of repairs and maintenance, discussed above in the section on tools, refer as frequently to the repair of stoves as to the repair of hearths or hearth furnishings. These statements tell us that the guardroom had a fireplace, and also mention "the fireplace in the second officer's bedroom," "the fireback in the commander's kitchen," and the two stoves of the "oven," probably the bakery.

The use of stoves shows the progress New France had made in the heating field.

> With such advantages, it is not surprising that the stove replaced the draw fireplace as the basic home heating device.... The edict of 1673 ... for safety reasons stipulated that stoves had to be located in fireplaces. However, by about 1725, the stove apparently became independent of the fireplace. Stovepipes now passed through partitions and floors, to circulate heat through the house.... The popularity of stoves continued to grow. In 1749 Kalm notes that habitants' houses along the road to Quebec were mostly heated by cast-iron stoves.... Stoves were also popular in the cities, and some middle-class people had more than one in their home.... However, the fireplace was not entirely eliminated by the popularity of the stove. Where the fireplace already existed, it survived, and people kept using it, especially for cooking....[21]

At this period, so-called "German" or five-sided stoves were used. These were fed through open backs and did not have pipes for smoke exhaust. There were also six-sided stoves that were completely enclosed and had exhaust pipes.[22] Stoves of the latter type must have existed at Fort Chambly because in 1731 Jean Fort *dit* Laforest, the locksmith, came to the fort to assemble three stoves and to make 24 feet of piping. And in 1733 he came to the fort "to fit the stove door."[23] The stove in question cannot have been of the "German" type, since that model did not have a door.

So-called "sheeted" stoves also enjoyed a certain popularity.

> The stove was placed in an opening made in the partition or dividing wall that separated the kitchen or the winter room (in country houses). This opening was covered with sheet metal. Small doors of sheet metal closed off the opening during the summer. In the winter, with the doors opened, both rooms could be heated at the same time.[24]

However, exhaustive architectural surveys at Fort Chambly have not turned up the least trace of such openings, nor have holes for exhaust pipes been found. (An exception is a hole in the roof of a vaulted chimney base in the cellar of one of the bastions. Presumably the cellar was heated by a stove whose exhaust pipe emerged through the floor of the hearth on the ground level, not a very suitable place. In any case, this haphazard arrangement would have been unsuitable for the upper storeys.) The absence of exhaust holes suggests that stovepipes were tied into chimneys, but since all Chambly's chimneys were destroyed, we cannot be sure of this. However,

their destruction could explain why no exhaust holes were found.

Any description of heating at Fort Chambly has to deal with a confusing document from the archives, a request made in 1759 by a M. de Roquemaure, who was stationed at Chambly. He asked to be lodged outside the fort because "there are only small stove holes in the fort. He claims that the stove is bad for his asthma."[25]

What are these "small stove holes" that de Roquemaure complains of? A hole could have been made in the fire-back of a hearth to allow a stove to heat two rooms. Such a hole might also have been made to feed a stove in the adjacent room. In both cases, however, the stove would have to be of the "German" type. Holes in walls could also have allowed pipes from a six-sided stove to pass from one room to another and thus provide radiant heat.[26] However, there are no such holes in the fort walls. Moreover, when Jean Fort *dit* Laforest came to Chambly to assemble three stoves and 24 feet of pipe, he presumably used eight feet of pipe per stove, which is not enough to allow the stovepipe to pass from one room to another.

De Roquemaure's enigmatic words raise two points. In the first place, he seems to be saying that hearths were no longer used in 1759. Secondly, his reference to "small stove holes" does not enable us to identify the model of stove used.

While there are many things that we do not know about the heating system at Fort Chambly, we do know that six-sided stoves (with doors and pipes) were used in conjunction with hearths well into the

1730s. The forges of St-Maurice produced stoves from 1742 on; from 1744 to 1746, 197 units were produced annually and were sold in the king's stores of the colony's three administrative districts.[27]

Lighting

Another aspect of material culture — lighting — is represented by an iron lamp of the so-called "cruzy" type, found in the fire stratum. Such lamps were in common use throughout the 18th century,[28] and this lamp almost certainly belongs to the period of the stone fort (Fig. 6). The cruzy lamp, a direct descendant of the oil lamps used in antiquity, is an oblong, flat-bottomed container, pinched at one end to form a spout that holds the wick. A handle is welded to the other end of the container so that the lamp can be suspended.[29] Robert-Lionel Séguin[30] described it as the poor man's lamp, which seems quite appropriate in view of its many drawbacks: "the light was very

6 Oil lamp, made of iron, commonly referred to as a "cruzy" lamp. (Photo by J. Jolin.)

feeble, the wick constantly crusting over and the odor of the burning fish oil anything but agreeable."[31] The fuel used in New France appears to have been seal or porpoise oil.[32]

Although the cruzy lamp was commonly employed by the farmers of New France and New England, it may not have been much used by the military. Income and expenditure slips for the years 1739, 1740, and 1741 show that several hundred pounds of candles were imported from France each year. In 1740, for example, purchases for Montreal included 200 pounds of candles and four copper candlesticks, but only two "iron lamps."[33] In 1749 the Shedaic detachment was sent 100 pounds of candles, two "iron lamps," two pairs of candle snuffers, and four clear hand lanterns with glass sides.[34]

Wax or tallow candles were also commonly made in tin moulds, at least in the homes of private citizens.[35] Candlesticks were made from copper,[36] pewter, brass wire, tin plate,[37] wood, silver,[38] and (as other archaeological excavations have shown) ceramic material.

At Fort Chambly various types of lighting might have been in use at the same time. Its occupants used cruzy lamps, of course, but also candles (as Hocquart attests) and lanterns. They may even have used torches, which they would have made themselves from wood chips and conifer resin.

Ordinary soldiers were only supplied with the necessities of life and would not have had candlesticks unless they made them themselves. On the other hand, officers likely brought candlesticks to the fort. Lanterns must have been used for outside illumination. However, architectural examination of the building has not determined whether or not lighting brackets were pegged into the wall. One fact is worthy of note: in the double latrines that were built in 1709 under the north curtain wall, a hollow, at a convenient height for a man, was made in the stone in each room. These hollows were presumably used to hold a candle or a lantern.

Furniture

Archaeological excavations rarely yield even fragments of furniture. Metal furniture fittings, on the other hand, are quite commonly found. But at Chambly, unfortunately, archaeologists recovered no furniture items dating to the French period of the stone fort. Consequently, all we can offer here is a brief overview of furniture based on primary and secondary historical sources. According to the regulations, at least as applied in Quebec, soldiers' rooms were furnished with a table, two benches, and as many beds as could be fitted into the space. The men slept two to a bed. The typical bed had an oaken frame, a straw mattress (replaced at least twice a year), a mattress filled with wool and covered with canvas, and a bed-head (the upper end of a bed) of the same material. According to Gilles Proulx, troops stationed at Quebec also had chests in which they kept their side arms and clothing. A transcript of a trial held in 1758 refers to a room in the attic of the New Barracks in Artillery Park, Quebec City, that was set aside for storing soldiers' personal effects.[39]

Fort Chambly's attic may have been put to a similar use, since in 1730 its lock was repaired. And in 1731 a lock was put on "a door to the attic." One of these locks was repaired in 1733.[40] However, the attic may have been locked simply because the commander or storekeeper wanted to protect provisions or supplies from theft. After all, one of Chambly's functions was to serve as a depot.

Around 1730 Chambly did have an icebox, a larder, an armoire, and "a small armoire in the guardroom."[41] The icebox and the larder were perhaps intended for the commander's or officers' personal use, or the storekeeper may have used them to keep food that was not yet distributed nor sold to the men. The small armoire in the guardroom must have contained articles used by soldiers on guard duty, such as lanterns, candles, overcoats, blankets, etc. The armoire with no specific designation cannot have been used in a barrack room. It may have belonged to the commander, to one of the officers, or perhaps to the sacristy. Then again, it may simply be the guardroom armoire, since the two wardrobes are mentioned in different documents.

Finally, two previously cited sources, Louise Dechêne and the inventory of the goods of the soldier Jacques Bonin dit Laforest (Appendix A), provide further information. Bonin dit Laforest owned no furniture, only "a canvas knapsack," which must have held his personal effects. The "bundle of old rags" he had acquired was contained in "a piece of cloth."

In discussing officers' furnishings, Louise Dechêne mentioned such items as an ebony cabinet, a chest covered with Moroccan leather, armchairs decorated with Hungarian needlepoint, an exotic rug, high-warp tapestries, chairs with cushions, cloth-covered tables, and feather beds.[42] The commander and officers of Chambly likely brought some furniture with them to make life more comfortable. After all, Chambly was closer to civilization than the trading posts to the west. It is difficult to state precisely how each man furnished his quarters, but very rare or very costly furniture surely could not have been taken to the fort: transport and the humidity of the place would have easily damaged them. Many officers had houses in town, and this must have influenced their choices as well. However, because of the humidity of the site and the risk of damage in transit, it is unlikely that very rare or expensive pieces of furniture found their way to Chambly. The fort probably contained such items as cozier beds than those supplied by the army, tables and chairs, and perhaps writing desks. The typical Chambly officer certainly had his own chest. He may also have had a pedestal table, an armchair, an armoire, and a travelling box or sideboard for his dishes. In addition, tapestries likely shielded him from the damp stone walls.

On the subject of furniture, the last word goes to the sieur de Sabrevois. When he was made commander of Fort Chambly in 1719 he asked the state for 500 *livres*. He wanted the money not only for the expenses associated with his office, but also for his appointments.[43] However, whether de Sabrevois was referring to the purchase of furniture and fittings or simply to the transportation of what he already possessed is not known.

Food

In archaeological excavations, food preparation and consumption is the best-represented human activity because it involves large numbers of ceramic and glass objects, which do not deteriorate. Though archaeological objects over-represent the food function, they do give us information on certain object categories seldom mentioned in another major source, post-mortem inventories of soldiers' effects. In these inventories the predominant items are textiles: clothing, bedclothes, towels, napkins, pieces of cloth, etc. For example, of the 33 items listed in the inventory of the possessions of Jacques Bonin *dit* Laforest (Appendix A, 25 or 26 if we count the silk wallet) are textiles. These inventories no doubt reflect the fashion-consciousness of New France's inhabitants in the 18th century.

Food-related artifacts account for a high percentage of the objects in our collection for each of the three forts and for the site as a whole. A detailed list of these items is presented in Table 8. Here the same functional divisions are used as in the preceding summary tables, but their contents are altered to represent significant assemblages more concretely. For

Table 8

Nature of Food-Related Objects from the Stone Fort

Undetermined use
- 17 coarse earthenware containers
- 1 refined white stoneware container
- 18

Getting food
- 2 iron fishhooks
- 2

Food preparation
Mixing or settling/separating
- 7 coarse earthenware containers
- 9 large coarse earthenware bowls or dishes with handles
- 4 coarse earthenware pans

Cutting
- 1 knife made of iron, brass, and wood
- 21

Cooking (in containers)
- 3 coarse earthenware cooking pots
- 1 cast-iron cooking pot
- 1 small cast-iron container
- 1 container made of sheet brass
- 1 large dish in brown tin-glazed earthenware
- 7

Storage
- 1 coarse earthenware butter dish
- 1 coarse earthenware jar or jug
- 1 hollow container of coarse earthenware
- 1 bottle of clear non-lead glass (common clear glass)
- 3 bottles of green-tinted glass
- 6 bottles of blue-green glass
- 1 bottle of blue-tinted glass
- 26 bottles of dark green glass
- 1 iron hoop from a wooden cask
- 41

Eating
Undetermined use
- 1 Italian coarse earthenware container (from Liguria)
- 1 container of coarse English earthenware (Staffordshire slipware)
- 2 tin-glazed earthenware containers
- 7 refined white stoneware containers
- 4 porcelain containers

Tableware
- 14 tin-glazed earthenware bowls
- 5 refined white stoneware bowls
- 7 porcelain bowls
- 6 bowls or cups of porcelain
- 1 plate of coarse English earthenware (Staffordshire slipware)
- 3 coarse earthenware plates
- 25 tin-glazed earthenware plates
- 13 plates of refined white stoneware
- 2 porcelain plates
- 1 small tankard of refined white stoneware
- 3 tin-glazed earthenware cups
- 1 cup or bowl of refined white stoneware
- 1 cup or bowl of porcelain
- 2 saucers of refined white stoneware
- 1 porcelain saucer
- 4 glasses made of lead glass (crystal)
- 3 glasses made of non-lead glass
- 4 lead-glass firing glasses
- 2 stemmed *verre fougère* glasses
- 1 stemmed glass made of lead glass

Table utensils
- 2 iron knives
- 1 knife or fork handle in iron and bone
- 1 folding knife made of iron and wood or bone

Serving dishes
- 1 tin-glazed earthenware serving dish
- 1 chocolate pot of coarse earthenware
- 1 mottled tin-glazed earthenware pitcher
- 2 lead-glass sweetmeat dishes
- 1 non-lead glass pitcher

Dishes belonging to soldiers' equipment
- 1 mess dish made of sheet iron
- 125

Total number of objects: 214

example, acquisition is included in the function of getting food. The storage and consumption of alcoholic beverages is also added, since it would be too restrictive to deal with them only under recreation.

Obtaining Food

Getting food was not a basic activity of soldiers since each man was entitled to a daily ration of bread, bacon, and peas, to which supplements were added. At Chambly, as in other military posts, the commander was likely entitled to buy food and sell it to his men. And the storekeeper must have run a canteen or beverage room where soldiers could buy and consume alcoholic drinks.[44]

At Louisbourg many soldiers were employed in building the fortifications, since it was hard to bring civilian manpower to Isle Royale. Soldiers could not buy on credit from the merchants of the town. Their captains therefore assumed the role of creditors, selling them tobacco, liquor, extra food, and shoes and stockings, which the king's ships never brought in sufficient quantities. These officers complained that their sales were reduced because the contractor who employed the men often paid them in consumer goods. Their efforts to monopolize this trade date from 1720, and from about 1730 to 1744 they received both the military pay and the civilian wages of the soldiers. They paid themselves a goodly portion of this money before distributing the remainder. They were soon paying the soldiers once a year, and opening canteens where

they sold wine and spirits on credit at exorbitant prices. Finally, about 1740,

> the French minister of the Marine expressed his concern about the "abuses" that were current in the garrison of Louisbourg. He thought that the situation there was much more serious than in the colony of Canada, which had long tolerated the officers' practice of appropriating their soldier-workers' wages.[45]

In 1749 Pehr Kalm[46] described the daily ration of a soldier at Fort St-Frédéric: two pounds of pure wheaten bread, lard, green peas, dried or salted meat, and sometimes fresh meat. At Quebec, at least, the ration was supplemented by a pot of molasses and a pound of butter once a month.[47]

This ration was hardly a gourmet's choice, especially when eaten every day, and the men of Chambly sought to improve their diet in various ways. The discovery of two fishhooks proves that they went fishing. Like fishhooks still in use today, these were made of a piece of iron wire that was bent and barbed at one end. The other end had an eyelet through which the line was tied. The hooks are quite long (5.5 cm and 5.25 cm) and were likely used to catch big fish. Invited to sup at Fort Chambly during his tour in 1752, Franquet noted that the menu included "all kinds of fresh fish of the best sort that are found in [the Richelieu] river, including bass."[48]

Analysis of fish remains at Chambly, in the form of bones, shells and scales, was conducted on the basis of minimum numbers of individuals.

This analysis has revealed traces of 20 channel catfish, 16 suckers, 5 sturgeon, 4 walleyes, 4 black bass, 4 fresh-water drum, 3 yellow perch, 3 fallfish, 3 pike, and 3 long-nosed gar.[49]

The occupants of Chambly also hunted. A document from the archives mentions that on 3 June 1715 a soldier returned from hunting at four o'clock in the afternoon.[50] Moreover, Kalm reported that the soldiers of Fort St-Frédéric could hunt and fish when they were not on guard duty. Kalm also mentioned that when moving from one place to another, officers could hunt water-fowl and trade fresh venison with the Indians in exchange for such items as ammunition and bread.[51] Some idea of what was bagged at Chambly can be obtained through the analysis of osteological remains: at least four muskrats, three red squirrels, three bears, two moose, two beavers, two martens, two stags, one hare, four turtledoves, three ducks, two buzzards, two crows, and several other wild birds of which only one specimen was found. (Beaver, because they lived in water, could be eaten on Fridays, when abstinence from other meat was required.[52]) This list of fish and game suggests that the inhabitants of Chambly had little difficulty in diversifying their basic menu.

Twenty-two parts of firearms were found in French contexts; five of these parts are associated with the stone fort. However, since it is difficult to attribute a given artifact to a military or a hunting musket, I merely noted the presence of these objects.

The remains of a number of domesticated animal species were also found. Since this meat had to be bought, it must have been eaten by the officers unless they sold it to their men. Archaeologists recovered the remains of at least 14 pigs, 11 cows, 10 sheep, 1 goose, 15 chickens, and 12 turkeys.[53] In 1758 General Montcalm had 50 sheep at Chambly.[54] The consumption of domesticated species is confirmed by the conclusions of the osteological report: "the overall impression is of dwindling hunting and fishing, and increased dependence on locally available domestic animals."[55]

On the subject of garden produce, Kalm chronicled that all the soldiers posted at Fort St-Frédéric cultivated a small garden plot on which they could even put up a tent. Kalm added,

> The commander informs me that this is a customary practice in all the fortresses held by the French in Canada when there is no large town nearby where green vegetables may be purchased.[56]

However, the men of Fort Chambly should have been able to buy fruit and vegetables, as well as dairy produce, from the inhabitants of the seigneury. Strawberries, raspberries, and blueberries were, no doubt, picked in season. And according to an expense sheet of the colony, two cows were bought from sieur de Lantagnac, the Fort Chambly captain, in 1735. This man must have owned and sold cows, and probably sold dairy produce as well.[57]

Collecting sweet maple sap to make maple syrup or sugar had been a common practice since the beginning of the 18th century. People quickly learned how to perform the various operations, such as tapping trees, collecting the sap, and reducing it by boiling. They also learned how to make sugaring cabins, occupied seasonally.[58] Kalm, our faithful reporter, tells us that both soldiers and civilians indulged in the sweets that nature had so generously supplied.[59] One can hardly blame them.

This rather scanty information gives some idea of what Chambly's occupants ate; however, much depended on circumstances. In peacetime they must have relied on nature, from sugaring-off in the spring to pumpkin harvesting in the fall. But we do not know to what extent Fort Chambly's inhabitants gathered nature's bounty or kept it through the winter months. Nor do we know how many preferred to buy produce from local farmers.

Individuals who lived at Chambly were thus able to enjoy a relatively diversified diet if they so wished. Fresh bread at least was available, since the fort had a baker. Rarer foods were also enjoyed, as is shown by the chocolate pot and sweetmeat dishes found on the site.

Preparing Food

Artifacts used exclusively for food preparation account for just ten per cent of food-related objects. This rather low proportion is explained in part by the fact that all containers used for cooking were excluded from this category. As well, fewer objects are needed to prepare than to serve food. One soldier could prepare food for a whole barrack room using a few good-sized utensils, and each man would bring his own place setting to the table. Chambly was not exactly a place where dainty dishes were lovingly prepared, as is shown by the nature of the artifacts. They are mostly multipurpose containers, like the large, flat-rimmed bowls that were found (Fig. 52 in Appendix E). Even the cooking pans, generally associated with separating milk and cream because of their smooth, brim-less sides and pouring spouts, may have been used to mix food.

The use of seven containers has not been determined. Since their rims have not been preserved, they cannot be classified as pans, large bowls, or basins. One thing, however, is certain: they are of no special form and are not designed for a specific phase of food preparation. Nine containers were made in France, and six appear to be of local manufacture. The latter were made, if not on the banks of the Richelieu, at least in New France.[60] These objects have simple forms, indicating workmanlike but not elegant manufacture. They are common objects with flared bellies, designed for a variety of uses. Two bowls show external traces of fire, the bottom of one being slightly blackened and the other blackened in places. This may indicate that they were used, if not for cooking, at least for reheating food or keeping it hot.

Jean-François Blanchette[61] cited the recommendations that a French chef, Marin, gave to the common people regarding utensils needed to prepare meals: glazed earthenware pots, pans, *huguenotes* (tripod cooking pots), saucepans and kettles of earthenware or copper, *coquemarts* (large kettles), silver platters, and even tin-glazed earthenware platters. The officers of Chambly may have possessed such items, but the men certainly did not.

Preparing food by cutting is represented at most by one knife handle. Though the handle may have belonged to a table knife, its trapezoidal tang and reinforcing strip suggest that it was used in the kitchen. The handle comprises two pieces of wood ("scales") held on either side of the tang by cuprous metal rivets. The rivet farthest from the blade secures the reinforcing strip, also of cuprous metal, which is joined to the end of the tang.

Osteological analysis shows that despite the little archaeological evidence of cutting tools, bovines were butchered at Chambly at the end of the French occupation. The remains of substantial cuts of meat, roasts in particular, were also identified for the later, but not the earlier, period.[62] From 1709 to 1760 Chambly's inhabitants used saws, knives, cleavers, and axes.[63] The sawing of carcasses was rather unusual, for this practice only became common at the very end of the 18th century.[64]

Cooking

In the preindustrial period, four methods were employed to cook food, especially meat and vegetables: roasting over an open flame, cooking in a container separating food from the source of heat, boiling, and braising or steaming.

In the first method, meat is cooked over an open fire on a spit or grill. In the second, fat is used to cook food in an iron or copper frying pan. The third method involves heating food that has been covered with water, utensils required for this being copper cauldrons or cast-iron cooking pots. Fourthly, steaming or braising is done by adding a cover to these two types of container, or by using a casserole, steamer, braising pan, or pie dish. This cooking method uses a cover to prevent steam from escaping, producing a moist environment inside the cooking container.[65]

Chambly's cooking-related objects include three ceramic cooking pots, one cast-iron pot, one small cast-iron container, one container of cuprous metal plate, and a brown tin-glazed earthenware cover.

The ceramic cooking pots may have been used for boiling, or for braising and steaming. One of these pots, typical of southwestern France, is pot-bellied and has a raised rim with two handles.[66] It is made of coarse earthenware and is only glazed on the inside. The mouth of the pot is 19.3 cm across, so that food could be easily placed inside it. Another pot, also of coarse earthenware, has a straight rim, an applied decorative handle, and glaze on the outside. Though it may have been used for storage, it was attributed to cooking because of its handle.

On account of its size, the brown tin-glazed earthenware cover may be attributed to a *huguenote* or a pâté dish (Fig. 7).[67] The use of such containers reflects the revolution in cooking methods that occurred in France in the mid-17th century and affected the 18th century as well. The noble and middle classes adopted a new form of "haute cuisine" featuring slow cooking methods,

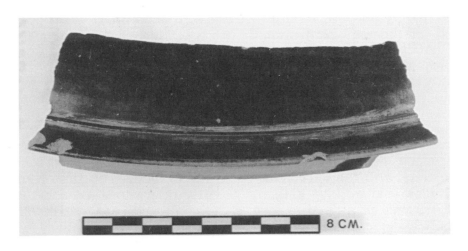

7 Brown tin-glazed earthenware cover
of a container used for slow cooking.
(Photo by J. Jolin.)

8 Part of a cast-iron cooking pot.
(Photo by N. Royer.)

which led to greater use of brown tin-glazed or coarse earthenware cooking pots.[68] Brown tin-glazed pots, which were more decorative, were preferred because they could be brought directly from the fire to the table. They were used to prepare soups, stews and, apparently, sauces, creams, and custards.[69] This new approach to cooking was popular mainly with the upper classes; the middle and working classes, through ignorance or a need to save money, only became interested in it at a later date.

The cast-iron cooking pot must have been about 20 cm high. Its opening was about 24.0 cm. It is a very simple model, easy to reconstruct. It has a straight, slightly projecting rim, triangular handles, and a bottom that is flat or slightly concave. It could have been a tripod vessel, with fluted legs and triangular pads, and it must have had a handle that was used to suspend it (Fig. 8). From its dimensions, it probably held enough food for about ten people. It is obviously associated with boiling.

I do not know exactly what use was made of the small cast-iron container represented by one small fragment. It may have been a cooking pot or a mortar.

Finally, this category of objects includes two fragments of sheet copper or brass pierced by rivets. These fragments, though they can be reassembled, form an irregular piece that may have been part of a container. Clearly identifiable remains of cuprous metal cooking pots were also found in the archaeological contexts of the first two forts. "Cuprous metal" is used to refer to a material that cannot be positively identified either as copper or as brass. Indeed, we do not know to what extent 18th-century people distinguished these two materials. A New England inventory mentions "a brass kettle" and "a copper kettle,"[70] which shows that the distinction was made. On the other hand, the terms "yellow copper" and "red copper" seem to have been used in New France. The first term apparently refers to brass and the second to unalloyed copper. The distinction is important where fairly heavy objects are concerned because of the softness of copper (for example, a copper candlestick would be weaker than a brass candlestick). In the case of sheet-metal objects, however, the difference is less important, since sheet copper was apparently as strong as sheet brass.

The container fragment is hardly representative of the number of these objects that existed in the colonies. The list of goods delivered to Shediac in 1749 mentions one iron cauldron as opposed to 30 cauldrons of yellow copper and 14 of red copper.[71] According to Séguin,[72] the copper cooking pot is an important trading item. At the St-Maurice forges, copper casseroles and cauldrons were used for heating water or even for cooking. However, the cooking pots were made of cast iron, as one would expect in such an area.[73] The popularity of containers made of cuprous metal may be explained:

> Early in the [18th] century, brass and copper were much costlier than iron, so much that the purchase of a kettle was worth special note in the diary of the Reverend Joseph Green of Salem who thus recorded the

major events of July 6, 1710: "Bought a brass Kettle, 3£/6 shil./6 p.; and went to Cambridge and brought my mother home with me at 6 o'clock." Brass and copper were worth the investment, however, for they had special advantages over less expensive ware; they could be dropped or clattered against one another and although sustaining dents, they did not crack and break as quickly as iron. The substantial numbers of brass and copper pots, kettles, and other utensils listed in colonial inventories are perhaps greater in ratio to similar accessories made of iron than is shown in restored kitchens today.[74] Copper is much lighter than iron or cast iron and is thus much easier to transport.

The description of the cooking function is very sketchy because it only represents about three per cent of the collection. That fact is, perhaps, our most important piece of information: cooking at Chambly was a straightforward business requiring little special preparation.

Eating

Eating, involving the use of tableware, cutlery, serving plates, glasses, and a certain number of multipurpose objects, accounts for nearly 60 per cent of Chambly's artifacts. But — for there is a "but" — the collection cannot be regarded as a unity because of an archaeological problem that requires some explanation. Most of the objects associated with eating come from two lots

of material that was used to fill in the latrines. The British apparently did this shortly after they occupied the fort in 1760, though the exact date is not known. Excavation of the latrines has recovered 36 French artifacts (one perhaps of local manufacture), 47 British objects, 23 pieces of oriental porcelain, and one Italian coarse earthenware sherd. Were the non-French objects brought to Chambly by French or British soldiers? Only a partial answer can be given. The osteological study reveals a substantial difference between latrine lots 16G8A32 and 16G8A36 and the other lots from the stone fort (in particular, the latrine lots contain many more turkey and chicken bones). Lot 16G8A43 poses the same problem, but in a less acute form since it comprises only five objects. Although these ambiguous lots contain objects in other categories, the problem is mentioned here because their artifacts in other categories are clearly French on the face of it, or are so isolated that they have little bearing on our overall interpretation. For example, lot 16G8A32 contains three objects in the tool category, but even if they were set aside, we would still be left with the fact that tools at Chambly are under-represented, and our interpretation of this category would not change.

The latrines' English ware, oriental porcelain, and Italian ware will be studied separately, then the French objects from all lots of the stone fort will be analyzed.

British Objects
Though the status of English glass and ceramic artifacts at Chambly is

problematic, I have not eliminated the objects because they date from the 18th century and may have belonged to French military men. An example is the lead-glass cup with glass pontil, which reflects a manufacturing technique primarily used before 1720.

From 1717 on, a royal order prohibited the sale in the colony of objects not manufactured in France.[75] The order reflected the colonialist policies of the time, which stipulated that colonies should supply raw materials to the mother country and provide an outlet for its manufactured goods. However, as court and government records show, not everyone complied with the order. In 1741, for example, a search carried out in the convents, churches, and private houses of Montreal revealed that 449 of the 506 establishments searched had English objects.[76] These items were likely procured in various, and primarily illegal, ways.

Some individuals were exempted from the king's order. Auteuil de Monceaux, for example, was a gentleman who had been exiled from the colony and had made a fortune in New York. Once pardoned, he was allowed to return to Canada with a cargo of English goods, which included ten boxes of cutlery and hardware, ten iron frying pans, ten fire-back plates, and six boxes of tin-glazed earthenware dishes.[77]

Many English objects no doubt entered New France by the back door. Around 1740, for example, the development of mass production enabled British industry to put large quantities of fine tableware on the market. The novelty of these goods probably made them very attractive,[78] and they may have been smuggled into the colony via the islands between France and England, whose ports were in an intermediate position and therefore more open.[79]

Indeed, smuggling between New England and Canada seems to have been a serious problem for the authorities. The major causes of this activity were apparently the proximity of the English colonies, the slow pace of commercial relations with France, and the higher prices offered for pelts in the English territories.[80] Indians and Frenchmen went to Albany and returned with goods to sell in New France. And merchants from Albany and New York often came to Montreal on various pretexts to trade their goods for beaver pelts.[81] However,

> the contraband trade centred upon Montreal, whence the furs were carried down the Richelieu to Albany. The chief intermediaries between the French merchants at one end, and the English and Dutch at the other, were the converted Iroquois of the Jesuit mission at Caughnawaga, and, to a lesser extent, the Indians of the Saint-Sulpice mission which, in 1721, were transferred from Sault-au-Récollet to the Lake of Two Mountains.[82]

Since smugglers used the Richelieu, Fort Chambly's garrison was responsible for curbing their activities. Two seizures of contraband at Chambly are on record. The first occurred in 1723 and produced eight large pewter basins, 24 spoons, two pewter cups, 21 stoneware crucibles, 19 pairs of wool-carding brushes and 41 pounds of cord for making hunting nets.[83] The objects yielded by the second seizure, in 1732, included 80 pounds' weight of pewter dishes.[84]

Other goods were also smuggled. Textiles in particular were much in demand in Canada.[85] Other smuggled items included silver coffee spoons and forks, table knives, pocket knives, gold buttons, buckles, boots, lace, gloves, and mittens.[86]

British goods thus circulated in New France during the 18th century. The men of Chambly were particularly well placed for gaining access to contraband. They were no doubt neither all smugglers nor all angels. Some contraband may have wound up at Chambly as a result of illegal activities: a smuggling expedition, items pilfered from seized goods, trafficking with the Indians, etc. These clandestine activities and the popularity of English goods in Canada explain why such items existed at Chambly under the French régime.

The assemblage found at Fort Chambly comprises the following objects (illustrated in part in Fig. 9):

1 refined white salt-glazed stoneware container, of undetermined type;
1 small coarse earthenware container, of undetermined type (Staffordshire slipware);
4 refined white salt-glazed stoneware objects, presumed to be bowls;
4 tin-glazed earthenware bowls;
1 coarse earthenware plate (Staffordshire slipware);
2 tin-glazed earthenware plates;
12 refined white salt-glazed stoneware plates;
1 small refined white salt-glazed stoneware object, presumed to be a tankard;
1 tin-glazed earthenware cup;
7 refined white salt-glazed stoneware objects, probably cups;
2 refined white salt-glazed stoneware saucers;
4 glasses, made of lead glass, of undetermined type;
4 lead-glass toasting, or firing, glasses;
1 stemmed glass made of lead glass;
2 lead-glass dessert or sweetmeat dishes.

What is astonishing at first glance is the large number of refined white salt-glazed stoneware objects (27 out of 47, or more than half). By about 1730 the technology for making dishes from that material had been developed. Plates and dishes of refined white salt-glazed stoneware were very popular between 1740 and 1760,[87] then were gradually replaced by other fine ceramics. However, in their hour of glory, they were a mark of refinement and prosperity, and in England they supplanted tin-glazed earthenware.[88]

Many objects of refined white salt-glazed stoneware were also found at Fort Michilimackinac. Stone believed that the undecorated pieces date to the end of the French régime. In discussing the objects decorated with moulded motifs of the same material or with cobalt blue designs, Stone mentioned only their British origin and did not say whether the French used them though they are contemporary with the undecorated pieces.[89] At Fort Chambly most of the refined white salt-glazed stoneware artifacts are decorated. Does this indicate greater luxury at Chambly, or rather a use later than 1760? That simply isn't known.

On the decorated refined white salt-glazed stoneware found at Chambly three techniques were used: hand painting, scratch blue, and moulding in the object itself. One object of undetermined type, which may be a cup and consists of two sherds, has a polychrome design — in green, brown, red, and probably yellow — that is hand-painted on the glaze. However, the motif cannot be identified. In the scratch-blue method, the design is incised on the piece and the incisions filled with cobalt blue. This technique, primarily used for cups and saucers,[90] is represented at Chambly by a fragment of a bowl or cup with arabesques on its outer surface and by part of a saucer (Fig. 9f) whose inner surface is decorated with arabesques and lozenges made of double lines. Patterns moulded in the object itself are of two kinds: linear hollow or relief mouldings running around the circumference of bowls, cups, or objects of undetermined type, and motifs specifically used for plate brims. One specimen of this technique at Chambly has a rim with an outer gadrooned fillet set off by two small inside fillets (Fig. 9a). Two others have rims with smooth outer fillets, the rest of the brims being executed in a barley motif. Finally, there are a number of objects with smooth outer fillets and series of motifs inspired by basketwork: a cartouche with beaded fret surrounded by foliated scrolls, a panel with interlaced design, and a cartouche with a star-motif fret.[91] These designs seem to have appeared around 1750.[92]

Refined white salt-glazed stoneware, though not a great luxury item, was very popular with people who could afford good tableware:

In view of its history and technology, white salt-glazed stoneware seems to represent an attempt to improve the hardness, whiteness, and texture of refined earthenware that, until that time, had been used in the manufacture of tableware.

The manufacture of refined white stoneware did not last very long, but it was an independent industry. Its products suited the popular taste of the time and were much in vogue in England and Continental Europe between 1740 and 1760. During the most active period of production, 1740-1780, many white stoneware items of this kind were exported to the colonies of North America.... This tradition certainly represents the highest degree of refinement reached in stoneware up to the 18th century.[93]

British tin-glazed earthenware is represented by seven objects, for the most part hollow containers. This ware was used at Quebec's Place Royale under the French régime, but was not available in as many forms as French ware of the same type.[94] In 1757, goods that a ship's captain transported to Louisbourg and St-Dominique included a "fine English tin-glazed earthenware and a crystal beaker."[95]

The British tin-glazed earthenware found at Chambly is all decorated, with varying degrees of success. However, no piece is complete with its design intact. The collection includes a plate and two

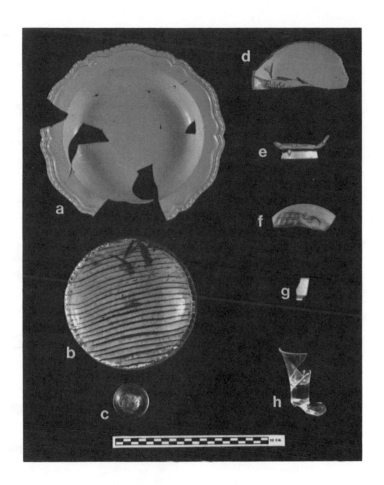

9 Objects of British origin, lot 16G8A32: a) refined white stoneware plate; b) coarse earthenware plate, "Staffordshire slipware" type; c) foot of a lead glass sweetmeat dish; d) tin-glazed earthenware bowl with fish design and (not shown) powdered decoration; e) small tin-glazed earthenware bowl; f) refined white stoneware saucer with scratch-blue decoration; g) small refined white earthenware cup; h) lead-glass toasting, or firing, glass. (Photo by J. Jolin.)

bowls with blue linear motifs (Fig. 9e), of which one is particularly crude, and a cup with floral decoration. Oriental motifs imitating porcelain designs are found on a bowl and a plate. These are decorated with guilloches and points within bands defined by two lines. The plate also has recumbent lozenges, and the lip of the bowl is set off by a brown line. The execution of these designs is, on the whole, rather hasty. The most luxurious piece is a bowl, which must have been rather large, since its foot is 8.0 cm in diameter. The bottom of the bowl has a fish design painted in blue (Fig. 9d), and the upper outside surface of the foot is decorated with a band of powdered purple. This band is repeated on the rim above a design of blue fish scales on a paler blue background. A complete dish with the same decoration, namely a blue fish and a powdered purple band, is preserved in the Daughters of the American Revolution Museum in Washington, D.C. This dish is dated to around 1740. According to J. Federico Taylor, "delftware plates with a wide rim coloured with powdered manganese were made at the Wincanton Pottery in Somerset and by factories in London, Bristol and Liverpool about 1740."[96] This type of powdered decoration dates from the 17th century. It must have enjoyed renewed popularity in the mid-18th century, when it was revived by all English factories.[97]

The Chambly assemblage also includes a coarse earthenware generally known as Staffordshire slipware. This is a beige ceramic fabric covered with white slip, decorated with lines of brown slip in resist, and covered with a yellowish glaze. At Chambly it is represented by a small hollow container of undetermined use and by a small complete plate. This type of ware is widely distributed on North American sites, but is not very remarkable for its quality.[98] One is struck by the strict simplicity of the shape of the plate (Fig. 9b), which has no foot, no brim, and only slightly concave sides. Its only decoration consists of festoons, probably hand-made, on the circumference of the thick rim. Staffordshire slipware, often found in French contexts, was in use in North America from the early 18th century.[99]

The latrine lots 16G8A32 and 16G8A36 also include clear glass objects whose English origin is shown by their form and by their lead content (they are, in fact, crystal). The objects include the bottom of a tumbler, which was blown in a pattern mould, producing a decoration of blurred vertical lines. The pontil on this piece would suggest a date prior to 1720.[100] Twelve fragments represent three objects that have been identified as the cups of stemmed glasses because of their straight, polished rims. We can associate them with a stem whose inner decoration is in the form of a

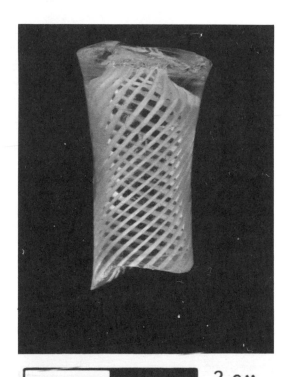

10 Fragment of lead-glass stemware, the stem having an opaque double-spiral decoration; of British origin. (Photo by J. Jolin.)

60

double white spiral. According to Ivor Noël Hume, this kind of stem dates to the period 1755-75 (Fig. 10).[101] Four stemmed glasses known as firing glasses are associated with the British custom of toasting. Each is rather stubby and has a thick foot, a short thick stem, and a flared cup.[102] This sturdy design allowed men to finish a toast by striking their glasses loudly on the table (see Fig. 9h). Firing glasses were very popular in the taverns of the American colonies. They were made from 1730 to the 19th century, but were most in vogue in the period 1750-75.[103] On a British military site, firing glasses can easily be attributed to the mess.

Finally, two stemmed sweetmeat glasses reflect another thoroughly British custom. These dishes (Fig. 9c) each have an open cup placed on a very low stem, here consisting of a large glass ball with hollow lozenges. The foot is slightly convex. Sweetmeat dishes were used to serve food that did not have a firm consistency, such as creams, custards, fruit compotes, and mincemeat, or food that was simply picked up and nibbled by the diners, like almonds. In well-to-do circles they were sometimes used for spectacular presentations of sugar sculptures, shaped pastries, moulded jellies, syrup fountains, etc.[104] While it is most unlikely that such elaborate efforts were made at Fort Chambly at any time in its history, the very presence of the sweetmeat dishes shows that its occupants sought some refinement. These dishes are our only British objects with a highly specific use. In England they were mainly in vogue at the end of the 17th and the beginning of the 18th century.[105]

Oriental Porcelain

All the pieces in the porcelain assemblage are of oriental, and likely Chinese, origin. Chinese items also account for 50 per cent of all porcelain-like material and 75 per cent of all hard-paste fine porcelain objects found on the entire site, in all contexts.[106] Since the European porcelain industry was still in its infancy in the mid-18th century,[107] the oriental artifacts could have been brought to Chambly and used either by the French or by the English. In any case, since they were luxury items, they almost certainly belonged to officers. Oriental porcelain, popular in the English colonies as early as the mid-17th century,[108] seems to have appeared at a later date in New France.[109]

At Fort Michilimackinac, porcelain is found mainly in English contexts, though the French also used it there from 1740 on.[110] The situation in the 18th century may be briefly described:

> During the 18th century, the China trade supplied increasing amounts of porcelain to Western Europe. Prior to the American Revolution, Chinese porcelain came to the colonies and Canada via Europe. There was no established trade between North America and the Orient. Chinese porcelain was imported quite early in the colonial period. Blue and white sherds of Chinese porcelain have been recovered in excavations at 17th century Jamestown, Virginia. By the mid-eighteenth century, Chinese porcelain

comprised an important segment of the China trade and was generally of good quality, yet reasonably priced. Though the secret of manufacturing both hard paste porcelain and soft paste porcelain spread through Europe from about 1700-1775, the Chinese porcelains remained competitive.[111]

According to Séguin, porcelain objects in New France included cups and saucers, sugar dishes, teapots, and cheese dishes.[112] And indeed, the 22 objects in the Chambly collection include a large number of bowls and cups, only two plates, and a few objects of undetermined type. This distribution is explained by the fact that porcelain was valued not only for its beauty and exotic nature, but also for its heat resistance.[113] One can thus associate porcelain with the consumption of hot beverages such as tea, coffee, chocolate, and even infusions of locally gathered herbs.

In 18th-century Canada even country folk drank coffee and chocolate.[114] Trade links with the Caribbean assured New France of a steady supply of these two products.[115] And one of the objects unearthed at Chambly is a coarse earthenware chocolate pot.

Porcelain bowls could have had various uses, such as serving condiments or sugar in small ones or even serving fruit in larger specimens. When employed in this way, porcelain was a symbol of status and wealth, giving its owner the same cachet as silverwork or jewels.

Oriental porcelains are traditionally classified according to the technique used to execute their designs.[116] In this classification, a distinction is made between underglaze monochrome blue patterns and overglaze polychrome enamel motifs. Whether blue or polychrome, designs were all painted by hand.

Polychrome designs are rarer because they are more expensive, requiring more skilled workmanship and manufacturing time.[117] At Chambly, for example, only three of 20 decorated porcelain pieces are polychrome. On one of these the polychrome effect is confined to red highlights on an underglaze blue design. The other two polychrome objects are small bowls with carefully executed floral motifs. One of these bowls has a design in red and green; the other, a pattern in green, yellow, and brown, with perhaps a trace of gilding (Fig. 11). Since most of the porcelain objects are only represented by a single sherd, blue decorative patterns are hard to identify. However, we can make out four floral designs, four landscapes, and four decorative bands with guilloches, the latter being a motif copied by English tin-glazed earthenware. Horizontal lines are often used to set off the hollows or parts in relief.

Oriental porcelain shows that there were luxury items at Chambly, but only to an extent that was typical of the rest of New France and even of the North American colonies as a whole.

Italian Ceramics

Only one sherd of Italian ceramic ware was found; its use cannot be determined. The sherd is typical of coarse Italian ceramic ware from Liguria. While this type of ware has not yet been precisely dated, it was

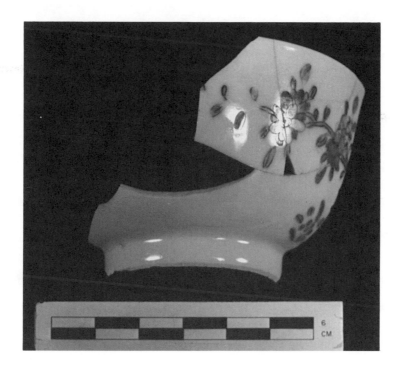

11 Oriental porcelain bowl with floral polychrome decoration. (Photo by N. Royer.)

very common on the Mediterranean coast of France and in northern Italy in the late 18th and early 19th centuries, and it was exported to the colonies, since many specimens of it were found at Louisbourg and Fort Beauséjour.[118] However, I cannot say for certain whether it belongs to the English or the French period. The sherd has no distinctive aesthetic or utilitarian qualities, and only its Italian origin makes it stand out from the rest of the ceramics.

French Objects

This section deals with the function of eating, using objects of French origin from lots 16G8A32, 16G8A36, and 16G8A43, together with artifacts from other archaeological contexts associated with the stone fort under the French régime. I have deliberately broken down the assemblage defined in Table 8 to present the French objects (Tables 9, 10 and 11).

These tables reveal two striking facts: the predominance of tin-glazed earthenware (74.1 %) and tableware, especially plates and bowls (68.0 %); and the remarkable, almost total absence of pieces with specific uses. Gérard Gusset noted the same phenomenon in the collection of salt-glazed white stoneware that he studied: "We only have objects for the most current and immediate uses. This choice may be due in large part to the military

Table 9

Nature of Objects of French Origin from the Stone Fort
Relating to Eating

Undetermined use

2	tin-glazed earthenware containers
1	hollow tin-glazed earthenware container
3	

Tableware

2	coarse earthenware objects, presumed to be plates
2	deep dishes of coarse earthenware
22	tin-glazed earthenware plates
7	tin-glazed earthenware bowls
3	tin-glazed earthenware objects, presumed to be bowls
2	tin-glazed earthenware cups
1	glass made of clear non-lead (common) glass
2	tumblers made of clear non-lead glass
2	grey *verre fougère* stemmed glasses
43	

Table utensils

1	folding knife made of iron and wood or bone
2	iron knife blades
1	knife or fork handle made of iron and bone
4	

Serving dishes

1	tin-glazed object, presumed to be a serving dish
1	mottled tin-glazed earthenware pitcher
1	coarse earthenware chocolate pot
3	

Total: 53

function of most of the sites excavated to date."[119] Men on garrison duty in a campaign fort like Chambly, even if they were officers, had to organize their environment along practical lines, and bring objects that could be used for several purposes. In 1753 Franquet considered himself to have been received at Fort Chambly and other posts with ridiculous pomp;[120] nevertheless, the proprieties must have been restricted by the material conditions of life in a fort of this type. It

Table 10

Materials Employed in the Manufacture of Objects of French Origin from the Stone Fort Associated with Food Consumption

Material	Objects	%
Tin-glazed earthenware	39	74.1
Coarse earthenware	5	9.5
Clear glass	3	5.7
Verre fougère glass	2	3.8
Iron	2	3.8
Iron and other	2	3.8

Table 11

Functions of Objects of French Origin from the Stone Fort Associated with Food Consumption

Material	Objects	%
Plates	26	49.0
Bowls	10	19.0
Total	36	68.0
Cups	2	3.7
Glasses	5	9.4
Utensils	4	7.5
Serving dishes	3	5.7
Undetermined use	3	5.7
Total	17	32.0
Grand Total	53	100.0

is even likely that coarse earthenware containers, classified above as preparation utensils, were used to serve food at the table. Officers may have used pewter or silver dishes, but such items rarely appear in archaeological excavations. Metal objects, because of their intrinsic value, were no doubt kept even when broken, if only to be melted down. They were not discarded in the latrines like ceramic ware, which lost all its value when broken, even if it were rare porcelain. In the inventories consulted, pewter containers were assessed by the pound, so what mattered was the amount of metal they contained.

Tables 10 and 11 reveal the low representation of drinking glasses. Chambly's occupants may have preferred metal drinking cups because they were unbreakable. The lack of table utensils is more difficult to explain. Pewter utensils were likely kept even when broken, as were other objects of the same metal. Steel or iron utensils would also be kept so that the metal could be reused. Besides, table settings must have been minimal at Chambly.

Of all the objects unearthed by archaeology, utensils are the least frequently found. When a utensil breaks, it can easily be modified to make another useful object. It is also possible that high-quality utensils were kept for a long time because of the value of the materials used in their manufacture.[121] The most noteworthy serving dishes are the pitcher and the chocolate pot. The pitcher is remarkable for its material: mottled tin-glazed earthenware with a purple-

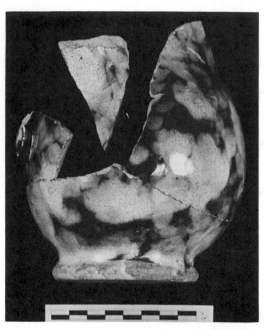

12 Pitcher of mottled tin-glazed earthenware, of French origin. (Photo by N. Royer.)

13 Coarse earthenware chocolate pot, of French origin. (Photo by J. Jolin.)

brown outer glaze shot through with irregular spots of white glaze (Fig. 12). The piece strongly resembles two pots from the Place Royale at Quebec. Their decoration, known as "candle drippings," perhaps originated in Nevers. One of these pots apparently dates from the second half of the 17th century, the other from the first half of the 18th.[122] Nicole Genêt indicated that this type of object is rather rare. Jean-François Blanchette illustrated a pitcher that is similar in form and decoration; however, his photograph is black and white, and the colour of the piece cannot be determined. He classified the pitcher as brown tin-glazed earthenware,[123] which means that it could have been placed over fire. The liquids most likely to be heated slowly are milk, cream, rum, and wine.

The chocolate pot is the opposite of the pitcher. Though made of rustic material, coarse earthenware, it has a highly specialized function (Fig. 13). While it could, of course, contain liquids other than hot chocolate, its use is very limited by its typical form: small dimensions, narrow pouring spout, cover, straight handle. To prepare hot chocolate, water was boiled in the pot. Chocolate was added and allowed to melt. The mixture was then whipped with a special stick (a *moulinet*), reheated over the fire, and poured into cups.[124]

Chambly's chocolate pot must have been used in this way, for its glaze has changed colour through exposure to flame. Though its special function suggests luxury, it is not remarkable in itself. Ceramic chocolate pots were not highly valued because, once heated, they kept the mixture boiling for a long time, thus removing some taste from the chocolate. Moreover, the bulging form of the piece was not the best; a truncated conical shape was preferred.[125]

Eleven objects of tin-glazed earthenware, nine of them plates, are apparently undecorated. Six, including five plates, each have only a blue band roughly traced in the hollow of the rim, which is very turned up (Fig. 14). This form, where the brim is so strongly curved, is extensively represented at Fort Chambly, with or without a blue band. Gênet referred to this as common tin-glazed earthenware,[126] which is most likely given the rather crude manner in which the blue band has been applied, which suggests cheap mass production.

Many of the tin-glazed earthen-

14 Common French tin-glazed earthenware plate decorated with a simple blue band. (Photo by J. Jolin.)

ware artifacts (14 objects, including 7 dishes, 6 bowls, and a cup) have blue designs, sometimes in two different shades. Most of the designs are floral; however, there are three imitations of Oriental motifs and a design in the Moustier style.

Finally, there are six objects (one plate, two objects of undetermined type, two bowls, and a cup) with polychrome decoration. Their designs are hard to identify because the fragments are small. The rim of the plate has a blue and black outlined band, likely the mark of the Rouen style. The colours used for this group of pieces as a whole are red, yellow, violet and, of course, blue. However, they are never all used at the same time.

The decorated objects, like the plates, produce the same general impression of hasty execution. Lines are often wavy and some motifs are blurred. Many small indications add up to a picture of hurried manufacture often seeming devoid of artistic merit. One could believe that France only exported low-priced products. However, New France did import high-quality tin-glazed earthenware from the mother country, as is shown by the objects of the Place Royale.[127] Fine pieces probably did not belong to military men or — which would probably be more accurate — were not brought to Fort Chambly lest they be damaged. Here again, practical considerations predominate. A diversity of the forms was available in tin-glazed earthenware: in 1757 a shipping cask might contain, for example, 4 dozen plates, 12 porringers, 51 water jugs of various sizes, 6 coffee cups, 12 handled cups, 6 candlesticks, 4 holy-water basins, a chafing dish, 5 salad bowls, 2 sauceboats, an oil cruet, an ink stand, 2 shaving basins, and 8 chamber pots.[128]

Only a few pieces of coarse earthenware are associated with eating. Of these, one burnt object, of which nothing can be said, must be eliminated. What is left are three plates, one apparently of local manufacture. The other two plates are interesting because their style is more elaborate than that of the other coarse earthenware pieces. One plate has a design in green slip on a background of white slip covering a red fabric. The other plate, of buff-coloured paste, has a green

2 CM.

15 Stem of a *verre fougère* glass. This specimen is from a context of the second wooden fort. (Photo by J. Jolin.)

16 Tumbler of common clear glass. (Photo by P. Vézina.)

17 Pocket knife decorated with wooden scales. (Photo by J. Jolin.)

glaze on the inside and on the outside a white slip covered with greenish translucent glaze. These pieces, or at least the one made of the red fabric, apparently come from southern France. Since similar objects were found in the cargo of the *Machault* and at Louisbourg,[129] the Chambly plate may date from the end of the French régime.

There is little to say about Chambly's glassware except that the *verre fougère* glass connotes luxury (Fig. 15). The other glass objects are rather common, including the almost complete tumbler decorated with vertical hollows created by blow moulding (Fig. 16).

On the subject of cutlery, pocket knives were most frequently used at the table. These were common knives that men kept on their person and put to other uses during the day. The pocket knife was the everyday handyman's tool. However, its importance must be qualified by the fact that in the archaeological collection of the St-Maurice forges, only 20 knives of a total collection of about 600 are of the folding type. However, the assemblage of knives represents the whole period of active occupation of that site — 1737-1833.[130] The Chambly specimen would seem to be a spring knife: "this type of knife, which was widely used, usually has a handle of bone or ivory."[131] The Chambly knife, which is almost complete, has wooden scales (Fig. 17).

Not Present: Pewter

Pewter objects are completely absent. While I have already offered an explanation of this phenomenon, I cannot simply skirt around the issue because pewter dishes formed a very important part of the material possessions of people in the 18th century:

> Pewter utensils are the most common and least costly of all. Sideboards and larders are filled with spoons, plates, porringers, tumblers, salt shakers, cellars, sauceboats, and serving dishes made of this metal.
>
> Pewter has one great advantage. If a pewter utensil breaks, the pieces can be gathered up and melted in a crucible. The molten metal is then poured into moulds and transformed into new pieces that take their place at the table.... A large number of plates, porringers, and spoons are manufactured locally with imported pewter. This is usually pewter from Cornwall.[132]

(The French text reads "Cornouaille," but it should not be taken to mean the Cornouaille region in Brittany. Séguin seems to have forgotten the final "s" in the French word for the English site.[133])

If one can believe post-mortem inventories of the time, the plates, spoons, tumblers, and dishes used by workers in the St-Maurice forges under the French régime were almost exclusively made of pewter.[134] Pewter was also popular in the English colonies:

By 1750, many workaday kitchen and table utensils, which in the last century had been carved or turned from chunks of maple and wild cherry or molded from carefully shaved sheets of horn, could be purchased made of pewter in all towns of any size.... Philadelphia pewterer Cornelius Bradford advertised in 1765 that at the Sign of the Dish he offered this varied and typical stock: "dishes, plates, basons, tankards, measures, tumblers, salt cellars, spoons, milk-pots, close-stool pans, block tin and pewter worms for stills, candle molds and bottle cranes."[135]

Two seizures of contraband goods carried out at Chambly yielded a significant quantity of pewter plate illegally imported from New England.

The evidence confirms the hypothesis that Chambly must have had pewter, probably in greater abundance than ceramic ware. Pewter dishes may even have been supplied to the soldiers, since pewter was both practical and popular.

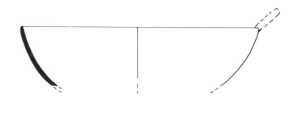

0   2 cm

18 Partial reconstruction of the iron mess dish. (Drawing by L. Lavoie.)

Eating on the Campaign Trail

A mess dish found at Fort Chambly represents the kind of equipment supplied for expeditions (Fig. 18). Since soldiers on campaign had to travel as lightly as possible, the mess dish is made of sheet iron, which was perhaps originally tinned. Sheet iron is both lighter than pewter and less expensive than sheet copper or brass.

The object has a very simple form, reflecting its eminently practical function, and is almost identical to modern mess tins. Because it is fairly deep and has a handle, it was no doubt used for cooking as well as eating. Twenty mess dishes were sent to Shediac in 1749;[136] however, the Chambly dish may be English, since it comes from latrine lot 16G8A32.

Storage

The storage category is represented by 43 specimens, of which more than half are containers for alcoholic beverages. The remaining objects have varied or undetermined uses.

One coarse earthenware object is thought to be a butter pot. Its origin is French and it is distinguished by its specific function. It could not have been used at the table given its large dimensions. Butter was probably purchased in large quantities and kept in the icehouse in tubs or pots. Tubs were imported from France.[137] Another object indicative of refinement is a liquor decanter (Fig. 19). Unfortunately, the 11 sherds that make up the remains of this piece cannot be assembled with enough precision to

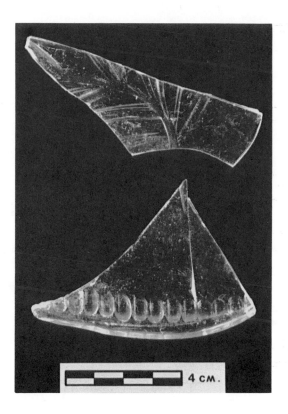

19 Fragments of a clear cut-glass decanter decorated with beads on the rim and plant motifs on the side. (Photo by J. Jolin.)

show its exact form. All that can be said is that the decanter was made of clear, non-lead glass, was rather tall, had four sides, was decorated with ovoid intaglio work on its edges, and had a foliate motif on two flat sherds. The butter pot and the decanter come from lot 16G8A32, but may be French.

Three identifiable jars and one object assumed to be a jar may have contained peas, salted meat, or anything else that had to be kept in large quantities. The three clearly identified jars come from the mixed contexts of the latrines. One of

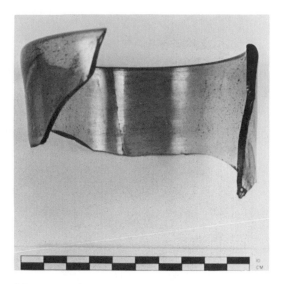

20 Opening of a French blue-green glass storage bottle. (Photo by N. Royer.)

21 Storage bottle of French blue-green glass. (Photo by J. Jolin.)

them seems typical of Biot, a factory in southern France, and another is of Canadian manufacture. The provenance of the third jar cannot be determined.

We also have a fragment of iron from the hoop of a cask, which seems to have had the same capacity as the jars. It is rather difficult to determine the cask's exact use, since it comes from lot 16G8A32 and could have contained foodstuffs or some other kind of goods.

The French origin of six bottles is shown by their particular blue-green colour. The form of these bottles varies according to the contents for which they were designed.[138] One bottle neck with a large opening (Fig. 20) must have been designed to allow the passage of olives, beans, pieces of marinated food, etc. A virtually intact bottle, which is four-sided and has a long neck with roughly finished lips, would have been used for olive oil or a syrupy liquid (Fig. 21). Some of these containers may also have been used to keep medical potions. To a greater extent than the large containers, these bottles can be associated with the officers' lifestyles.

The bottles used to keep alcoholic beverages — beer or wine — were almost all found in the latrines and are all of English origin. Represented by several hundred shards grouped into 26 objects, they are easily identifiable by their size (more or less the same as that of present-day bottles), their deeply

22 Green glass bottle for alcoholic beverages, of British origin. (Photo by N. Royer.)

indented bottoms, and their very dark green colour (Fig. 22). The fact that these bottles are of British origin is not, in this context, as significant as in the case of the refined white stoneware, for example. In the 18th century, France was unable to produce enough bottles to contain its entire production of alcoholic beverages, and therefore imported bottles from England.[139] It thus often happened that English containers arrived in New France carrying French contents. However, it would seem that most alcoholic beverages were exported in barrels and bottled in the colony.[140] According to Jacques Mathieu,[141] rum traded between the Caribbean and New France was shipped in casks. This is, indeed, the most sensible form of transportation if one wish to avoid breakage.

The Chambly bottles may have contained wine or, under the British régime, beer. In New France the most popular alcoholic drink was apparently wine, whether French, Spanish, or Cypriot.[142] Love of the grape affected most of the population, and even the habitants were very fond of wine, though they also drank beer, hard liquor, and a little cider.[143]

Finally, three bottles from lots 16G8A32 and 16G8A43 are so fragmentary and from such uncertain contexts that their use and origin cannot be determined. The pontil mark on the bottom of one ordinary glass bottle suggests a date prior to 1720. The other two bottles are represented by green-tinted fragments from the rounded parts of bottles. These pieces are much lighter in colour than bottles used for alcoholic beverages. The assemblage of the stone fort under the French régime contains two other bottle sherds, but these are much more recent in appearance and are, no doubt, intrusions.

Summary and Analysis of Data on Food

The common soldiers of New France had to endure a repetitive diet. This is shown conclusively for the Quebec City garrison, whose members were at least able to frequent the city's cabarets.[144] What must things have been like at Chambly? Fortunately, its inhabitants had enough time on their hands to go hunting.

According to Blanchette,[145] officers were scarcely better off: "the diet of the military [officers] of the time ... consisted mainly of soups, stews, bread and drinks," yet the Chambly officers were able to offer Franquet a real feast.

Food at Chambly was probably not all that bad. While the fort's occupants obviously did not enjoy sumptuous feasts in the dead of winter, they must have done what they could to improve their ordinary fare by using the resources of the environment, which were abundantly available.

However, Chambly's assemblage of food-related objects shows that its inhabitants did not go to elaborate lengths to prepare, cook, or serve food. These artifacts are mostly multipurpose and of common manufacture. An exception to this rule would be the oriental porcelains and British ware of lots 16G8A32, 16G8A36 and 16G8A43, if we choose to include them in the artifacts used by the French. These objects do reflect a certain desire for luxury, but are still quite unspecified as to function. While the problem of attribution does not admit of any definite solution, Chinese and English ware probably did grace the tables of Fort Chambly's French occupants. The British items in question consist mainly of bottles and tin-glazed earthenware.

Few small storage containers were found, which suggests that condiments and oil were not much used at Chambly. Food was probably cooked in butter or animal fat and seasoned with the usual imported spices or locally gathered herbs. Hocquart's letter to the minister in 1734 does mention oil in the king's stores, but does not say what kind it was.

Chambly's artifacts cannot, on the whole, be attributed specifically to officers or to men. However, as already noted, common soldiers probably did not own many ceramic or glass objects. Those who had only their military pay could not afford them, and those who worked for civilians likely preferred to save their money or to spend it on something other than dishes. Indeed, it is hard to imagine common soldiers transporting plates and pans in their knapsacks. Officers were in better positions to pack and ship such items, which their men would carry for them in travelling boxes. Furthermore, most officers came from well-to-do families or were themselves involved in trade and thus had more substantial incomes. In moving to Chambly, they no doubt took along a few elegant pieces. They would have bought them or taken them from their principal residences, but the pieces would have been ones whose loss they would not have overly regretted.

Hygiene and Medical Care

Hygiene

In dealing with the subject of hygiene, one has to set aside the prejudices of our own time. Cleanliness is a very relative notion that varies greatly from era to era and from culture to culture. One thing is certain: our own criteria do not apply to the 18th century.

Regarding the workers at the St-Maurice forges under the French régime, Luce Vermette wrote:

> The difficulties associated with the supply of water ... suggest that personal cleanliness was at best a cursory affair, scarcely going beyond wetting the hands and faces and drying them with a linen towel.[146]

If the St-Maurice workers' standard of cleanliness was the norm, what should one make of Governor Duquesne's charges that the soldiers of Quebec were dirty?[147] The state provided each man with two pounds of soap and two combs per year, and "encouraged them to take regular baths" during campaigns.[148] Did the men of Chambly avail themselves of the waters of the Richelieu? Probably not to any greater extent than weather permitted and custom enjoined.

Archaeological excavations at Fort Chambly tell us little about cleanliness. Latrines were found, and four chamber pots. The latrines, located in the basement of the north curtain wall, were well constructed. Water could be poured from the courtyard into the latrines through an ingenious system of pipes so that waste would be washed into the river. Thanks to this arrangement, Chambly's latrines were likely more salubrious than many others of the time. The occupants of Chambly must have been able to enjoy basic sanitary facilities in relative comfort, at least when the latrines were not flooded by the river.

Two of the four chamber pots are English and come from latrine lot 16G8A32. Of the two other pots, one is of tin-glazed earthenware and one of coarse earthenware. Despite the difference in quality, both articles no doubt belonged to officers, since there is no reason to believe that common soldiers used chamber pots. While it may seem surprising that only two French chamber pots were found, most items of this kind are found in latrines, having slipped out of someone's grasp while being emptied. While the fort was in use, anything dropped into the latrines would have been automatically washed into the Richelieu by the sewer system.

To round out the account of toilet articles, the soldier Bonin *dit* Laforest possessed a horn comb in a sealskin case,[149] and the officer Joseph Déjourdy, sieur de Cabanac, had in his room in Montreal a tin-glazed earthenware chamber pot, a case containing two razors, a whetstone and a piece of leather, a tin-glazed earthenware shaving basin, a small mirror, a clothes brush, a pound of soap, and a powder puff.[150]

23 Phial for pharmaceutical products, made of green-tinted glass. (Photo by J. Jolin.)

Medical Care

Medical care, despite its importance, is no better represented than hygiene in the material culture of Fort Chambly. Here again one has to be careful not to project 20th-century experiences onto the past. While a large variety of prepared medications is readily available today, this was not always so.

Four phials came from latrine lot 16G8A32 (Fig. 23). One phial appears to be English since it is made of lead glass. Pontil marks show that one of the other phials was made before 1720, and that a third

is typically French. (Some blue-green glass fragments or objects attributed to food storage could have been used to keep pharmaceutical products.)

The phials are long and cylindrical in shape, and are made of rather thin glass. The only remaining neck is short and is bent outwards at right angles to form a flat, circular rim. Phials of this type were usually kept in cases designed to keep them upright so that the potions, unguents, and pomades they contained would not spill.

Drugs were probably controlled by the fort's surgeon, whose presence is attested by historical documents for 16 years between 1719 and 1760. This does not necessarily mean that no surgeon was at the fort during the years that are not mentioned in the documents.[151] One must be careful to distinguish between doctors and surgeons.

> Surgeons, who practised their trade without speaking Latin, were lumped in with barbers. In the eyes of physicians, they were no more than contemptible helpers. They were controlled and obedient: simple labourers within the medical hierarchy. They also had to declare their allegiance before the assembly of regents once a year.[152]

The lot of surgeons improved in the mid-18th century, when they were deemed equal to doctors in the eyes of the law.[153] However, this reform probably occurred too late to have much impact on the situation in Canada before the Conquest. The fact of the matter is that in 1719 Chambly's surgeon was an 18-year-old common soldier.[154]

For some years at least, the nuns of Montreal's Hôtel-Dieu acted as apothecaries for the men of Chambly. In 1736, 1737, 1739, 1740, and 1742, drugs were bought from them for use by the garrison of the fort.[155] In particular, 708 *livres* 15 *sols* worth of drugs were ordered in 1736. This very large amount can probably be explained by the epidemic of smallpox that raged through New France that year.[156] For the other years, drug purchases varied between 119 *livres* 10 *sols* and 154 *livres* 8 *sols*.

Drugs in use in the 18th century can be roughly divided into four categories: vegetable products, animal extracts, derivatives of metallic products, and prepared medications, such as elixirs and pills.[157] Appendices C and D present two drug lists. The first, which dates from 1688, is a statement of "necessary medical supplies that must be procured from France for the troops in Canada." The second is taken from an advertisement that appeared in 1769 at Williamsburg. Though the second list is longer, many items are the same on both. It would be most interesting to study these lists in detail and to relate them to the history of medicine. In the mind of the non-expert at least, they raise many questions. Many are quite familiar with the uses to which cassia and senna were put, but know much less about the medicinal properties of, say, mastic. And the nature of a number of products, like cornachine powder, is completely unknown.

In his research on the soldiers of Quebec, Gilles Proulx found only a few mentions of disease. These included scabies, rheumatism, consumption, hernia, partial blindness, chest pains, insanity, and epilepsy.[158] In addition to the wounds associated with their trade, the troops no doubt suffered as well from such widespread diseases as influenza, smallpox, typhus, and malignant fevers.[159]

Clothing

Since the military uniform of the time is well known, it need not be described in detail. The soldier's "outfit" consisted of a coat, jacket, and breeches, to which were added a shirt, stockings, shoes, and a hat. Such uniforms were supplied to the soldiers, but deductions were taken from their pay to amortize the cost.[160] (In 1747 the garrison at Fort Chambly received 30 pounds of deerskin, 40 pairs of shoes, and 40 pairs of oxhide shoes.[161]) Since soldiers could not wear their uniforms when involved in non-military work or activities,[162] they also required civilian clothing. This is confirmed by the inventory of the possessions of Jacques Bonin *dit* Laforest (Appendix A).

Textiles are not, of course, preserved in the ground and are thus absent from the archaeological collection. However, excavation revealed two buttons and the remains of a piece of braid, which seem to have belonged to the uniform of a member of the *Compagnies franches*. The objects are made of cuprous metal, corresponding exactly to what is said about this trim in the historical record, which speaks of copper buttons and gold-coloured braid (probably made of so-called false gold.[163]) One button is very similar to a type found at Michilimackinac in a context dating from the period 1740-60. This specimen has a crown, a rounded back, and an eyelet formed from a small strip of metal. The buttons from Michilimackinac bear traces of silver brazing on their backs and have concentric grooves on most of the crowns.[164] The buttons found at Chambly share these characteristics, though the other Chambly button is smaller and more spherical (Fig. 24). The piece of braid is more difficult to describe. One can discern the remains of yellowish fibres whose surface is tinged with green, probably through corrosion of the small strips of cuprous metal with which they are intertwined.

In the historical period on which this report focusses, the sword was a weapon of secondary importance, more in the nature of a status symbol.[165] Chambly yielded two remains of swords: the handle of a brass hilt, similar to the handle in Figure 51 in Appendix E, and the central part of the body of an iron hilt (Fig. 25). These are very common, mass-produced items used by soldiers rather than by officers. Officers had their own weapons, which were often highly decorated.[166]

Excavations at Chambly also uncovered a fragment of brass buckle, probably for a shoe or belt, and the

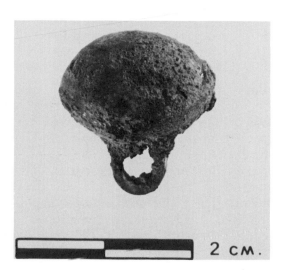

24 Button of cuprous metal, probably associated with military dress. (Photo by J. Jolin.)

25 Central part (ricasso, crosspieces, and hand guard) of an iron sword hilt. (Photo by J. Jolin.)

back of a wooden button, but whether these objects were used for military or civilian clothing cannot be determined. A small mother-of-pearl button with two holes may have graced a fine shirt.

In quality and nature, civilian garb at Chambly was no doubt much the same as clothing worn by Canadians in general. Canadians had a reputation for being crazy about clothes, and Kalm thought Montrealers much more stylish than their British neighbours.[167] Indeed, workers in the St-Maurice forges were accused of wearing too sumptuous clothing.[168] And the habitants dressed "in the French style" (i.e., in imported clothing) at least up to the mid-18th century.[169] However, the wardrobe of Bonin *dit* Laforest is not too elegant. In this as in all things, people had to live according to their means.

Recreation

Recreation has already been mentioned in the discussions of hunting, fishing, and alcoholic beverages. Hunting and fishing can be considered as a form of recreational sport even if their aim is to procure fresh food. In any case, they were certainly not onerous tasks.

The consumption of alcoholic beverages, certainly not limited to mealtimes, is a form of entertainment or pastime. At Fort Chambly, as elsewhere, the storekeeper must have run a canteen[170] where the precious nectar was sold. In 1751 the commander, de Muy, prohibited this practice[171] for reasons that are perhaps reflected in Duquesne's comment of 1753:

> There is another very important subject that has often concerned me. I am speaking of the soldier who has spent three or four years at a post and has returned penniless and in debt because the storekeeper supplied him with drink on credit, using the fellow's pay as collateral. Captains had to face advances they could not meet, and were obliged to leave

their soldiers in a state of great uncleanliness.[172]

Then as now, alcohol fumes often mingled with tobacco smoke. At Chambly 33 pipes were found. Made of fine white clay, they are basic pipes with simple shapes. They probably came from France and Holland. Many pipe-stem fragments resemble those found at Louisbourg:

> An unresolved problem regarding pipes of the kind illustrated in Figure 30 ["stem fragments showing rouletting bordered by a line of impressed triangles, probably Dutch"] ... is their indifferent workmanship compared with other Dutch material. These pipes are certainly not English, and some of this type from other parts of Louisbourg bear marks known to have been in use at Gouda at this time. Further, the parts of the bowl that survive, as well as the style of decoration, indicate Dutch inspiration. Dutch pipes, however, are consistently of a more refined workmanship than English pipes.... The types shown in Figure 30, however,

are markedly inferior to the example of the lower classes [of Gouda pipe] and it is possible that they may have been either crude imitations of Gouda pipes made elsewhere in The Netherlands, or perhaps in the Pas-de-Calais area of France, or in modern Belgium whence the Dutch obtained some of their clays.... Alternatively, these pipes may simply have been shoddy goods made, rather like glass beads, especially for selling to hapless overseas buyers.[173]

These pipe stems are typically decorated with impressed patterns of triangles and circles in rows, and with rouletted lines made by a

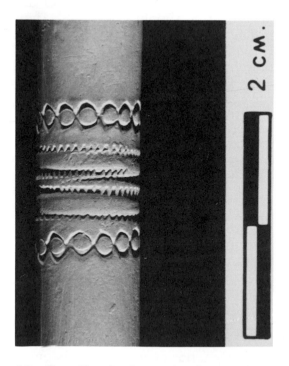

2 CM.

26 Detail of pipestem decoration, of French or Dutch origin. (Photo by J. Jolin.)

toothed wheel (Fig. 26).[174] The examples found at Fort Chambly have been rather crudely executed. The designs are impressed with varying degrees of success, the rouletted line is often crooked, and the pressure on the wheel has fluctuated. Whether these pipes be Dutch or French, they are indeed mediocre. Since such pipes have been found both at Chambly and at Louisbourg, it would be interesting to know whether they were sold mostly to the military or to all social groups in the North American colonies. Specimens of this type found at Michilimackinac bear the Gouda mark, date from 1715 to 1735, and are associated with the French occupation of the site.[175]

The pipe bowls in the Fort Chambly collection are not decorated, which confirms our impression of cheap, inelegant products. Some bowls that bear the manufacturer's mark can be identified as Dutch or English. One outstanding specimen (Fig. 27) has a bowl whose lip is decorated with light, oblique hatch marks incised by a toothed wheel, and has a stem moulded in a pretty cable design. This pipe is attributed to Dutch manufacture.

It seems likely that tobacco was bought at the king's store. Soldiers, or at least those in Quebec, received one pound of tobacco a month.[176] In the 17th and 18th centuries tobacco use was widespread, and some boys started smoking at the age of ten. Tobacco was also taken in the form of snuff, which was very popular in the 18th century, particularly among aristocrats and at the French court.[177]

In Canada, tobacco was commonly grown. The habitants grew it for

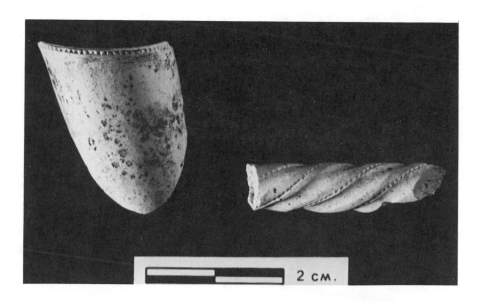

27   Pipe with braided stem. (Photo by J. Jolin.)

their personal consumption, but the quality was not always the best.[178] The Richelieu valley was well suited for growing tobacco, which was extensively cultivated by the mid-18th century. Hocquart even thought of growing it on a large scale.[179]

Tobacco was kept in various kinds of containers. The only tobacco container found at Fort Chambly is a bottle made of very dark green glass (Fig. 28). Bottles of this type were eight-sided and had very short necks and rather large mouths. They were, of course, used for storing tobacco, unlike the snuff boxes that were carried on one's person. Similar bottles are in the Louisbourg collection.

Gambling is a form of entertainment that often accompanied the consumption of alcohol and tobacco.

From the 17th century on, civil servants, coureurs de bois, officers, and men indulged in frenetic gambling, even in posts that were the farthest removed from Quebec and Montreal. Wages and military pay, earned through such risk and labour, were swallowed up in the random dance of cards and dice. For the colony's administrators this must have been a rather disquieting situation.[180]

A revealing post-mortem inventory of a soldier who was killed in a duel in 1722 informs us that the man's pockets contained three gambling dice, a knife, a pipe in a case, a "Job's-tears" rosary, and a pack of cards.[181]

Games of chance were all the rage in the 18th century; however, this popularity was not a sudden phenomenon. Have not all cultures, from the most ancient to the most modern, used gambling to help people forget life's cares?   In early 18th-century France the most popular card games were *hoca*, *biribi*, *dupe*, faro, basset, lansquenet, reversi, and brelan.[182] These were games of pure chance, requiring neither skill nor memory. Like the games of modern-day casinos, their sole interest lay in the stakes that were wagered. *Hoca* and *biribi,* which require special tables, were probably not played at Chambly (see Veyrier).

Gambling at Fort Chambly is illustrated by just one object, which comes from the fire layer. It is a die made of bone on which the numbers are represented by drilled points (Fig. 48 in Appendix E). However, there must have been many cards and dice at Chambly during the period of the stone fort. Three dice similar to the Chambly specimen were found at Michili-mackinac.[183] These objects may have been made by the soldiers themselves.

Finally, one should not forget pets, like Bonin *dit* Laforest's little dog. Perhaps it was also his hunting dog.

28 Part of the octagonal side of a tobacco bottle (Photo by J. Jolin.)

CONCLUSION

An assemblage of archaeological objects cannot be studied apart from the historical documents that situate them in their various contexts. Archaeologists unearth remains of material culture that have been rejected, forgotten, or abandoned, and may be able to explain why these have been buried in the ground. However, they must go further, not only to explain the use of objects, but also to locate them in their social, economic, and cultural contexts. For example, even if we decide to stress the history of objects, we have to retain human history as a backdrop, since one would not exist without the other. To get the most out of the ancient objects that have come down to us, we naturally have to document, date, and classify them. However, compilations of data are not ends in themselves. They are just another means of grappling with the problems of historical inquiry.

To deal with these problems, we need to have the right tools and knowledge in the fields of natural science, archaeology, ethnology, and the history of traditions and mentalities. In short, we need to master the sciences and techniques that improve our understanding of people in their environment. In this respect, this research report is rather tentative, since it is based on work undertaken with other objectives in mind: the archival material I consulted had not been organized with this report in mind, nor have I tried to provide a comprehensive interpretation of the various strata on the site. What I have done is to make the best use I could of data embedded in analytic frameworks not my own. In any case, the research work to date has been fascinating; it is a great satisfaction to breathe life into objects to which our ancestors once gave life and soul.

What, then, have we learned about the domestic life of Fort Chambly's occupants under the French régime, especially between 1709 and 1760? Statistical analysis of artifacts has taught us that the break of 1702, marked by the burning of the first wooden fort and the construction of a new palisade, coincides with the dawn of a more prosperous era in New France. This is indeed a coincidence, as there is no reason to believe that the first fort was deliberately burnt so that a more comfortable one could be built in its place. However, the rapid erection of the second fort shows that continual military occupation of the site was still necessary and that enough ready cash was available to cover the required costs. It was also a time of transition, when pioneers gave way to colonizers. This development, which continues during the period of the stone fort, is reflected in the assemblages of artifacts, where we find a greater diversity of functions and materials.

The objects from the stone fort have been described in detail and the fort, as it were, has been furnished. Simplicity, if not rusticity, is the hallmark of this material environment, suggesting a rather modest standard of living. There is, however, the matter of the British artifacts that were found in the latrines. If they really belonged to French military men, they are significant because they were forbidden and therefore less common. Lead glass, fine stoneware, and oriental porcelain are also more noble, more refined materials. While some of the problem British artifacts may date from the later years of the French régime, the luxury they reflect hardly existed for the whole period from 1709 to 1760. On the other hand, the French at Chambly certainly used porcelain at quite an early date, though to what extent is not known. However, even if Chinese porcelain and English tin-glazed earthenware are added to the collection, it still remains rather modest overall.

The poverty of the common soldiers at Chambly is not surprising. They were no better off in other posts. But what of the officers? Here points of comparison are lacking. Louisbourg, whose artifacts are richer and more diversified, was a port; the people who lived there had easier access to goods brought by sea. Moreover, Louisbourg was a small town inhabited by a large number of officers, who perhaps tried to outdo one another. The artifacts of Michilimackinac are similar to those of Chambly in quality, but differ in quantity, since Michilimackinac was a larger establishment with more varied functions. Because Chambly was a campaign fort in a rather isolated, sparsely inhabited rural area, it cannot be compared to the other French military establishments along the Richelieu, nor to the civilian or seigneurial structures in the vicinity. Yet, in spite of the inevitable lacunae in the research, the results of this study shed a brighter, clearer light than previously illuminated life on the Richelieu.

APPENDIX A

Inventory of the Possessions of Jacques Bonin *dit* Laforest

Inventory of the clothing and other personal effects belonging to Jacques Bonin *dit* Laforest at Chambly, including what he wore at the time of his arrest for theft. His property was handed over to the sieur de la Branche, who was responsible for the conduct of Bonin *dit* Laforest and for his trial at Quebec.

A wallet covered with silver-threaded silk brocade containing the following items: five 40-*livre* notes, two 7-*livre* notes, one 4-*livre* note, one 40-*sol* note, and two 20-*sol* notes; a silver ring set with an artificial diamond; one nail sharpened to a chisel point

A black cloth overcoat

An old hood of mazamet

A small, old coverlet

Six nightcaps

Four neckties

One woollen nightcap

One small, ticking-covered down pillow

One sealskin case containing a horn comb

A piece of Dourgne cloth

A pair of old canvas breeches

Two pillowcases

Two pounds of lead and bullets in a leather bag

A pistol

A canvas knapsack

Four shirts

A small parcel of old clothes wrapped in a piece of cloth

Quebec (Prov.). Archives nationales (Montreal), Archives judiciares, the king vs Jacques Bonin *dit* Laforest, sergeant in the *Compagnie d'Esgly,* 19 February 1716.)

APPENDIX B

Post-Mortem Inventory of Joseph Déjourdy, Sieur de Cabanac*

A leather-covered trunk with lock
Four old hair bows [?] ___
A deerskin-covered case with lock
A small cabinet
Two [glass] bottles
Another wicker bottle cover
A tin-glazed earthenware chamber pot
An old kettle of red copper
A case containing two razors, a stone and
  a strop
A tin-glazed earthenware shaving basin
A small mirror
An old lantern
A curved knife
A file ___
Two collar studs (silver)
The hook [scabbard clip?] of a sword
  (silver)
A spring knife
A pair of copper buckles
A pair of silk garters
A collar of ___
A clothes brush
A Malacca cane with coconut head
A pound of soap
Three old wigs à course

One cellar containing nine pint bottles
A red copper cooking pot with its cover
A wooden box and dish
A powder puff
A bark case
A large silver ___ musket
An old scabbard
A holster pistol
A pocket pistol
A medium-size axe
A hunting horn filled with powder
A powder flask
Two bags containing two pounds of lead
A small wooden table with leaf
A straw mattress and a feather bed
  covered with ticking, a wool mattress
  covered with checked ticking, a bolster
  and two pillows made of ticking and
  filled with down, a white woollen blan-
  ket and a green woollen blanket, a cot-
  ton quilt
A pine chest
A trunk
A case
An old rug of blue cloth
Two pairs of bedsheets

---

*Clothing not included.

Quebec (Prov.). Archives nationales (Montreal), Greffes des notaires, Greffe G. de Chèvremont, Inventory of property in the estate of Joseph Déjourdy, sieur de Cabanac, lieutenant, 27 March 1737.

APPENDIX C

Drugs and Instruments Ordered in France for the Troops in Canada, 1688

Theriace
Preparation of hyacinth
Preparation of Thermes
Preserved juniper
Water of theriaca
Water of blessed charcoal
Essence of anis
Opiate of Solomoni
Preparation of hamamelis
Diaphenia
Fine catholicon
Cassia
Senna
Anis
Rhubarb
Clyster catholicon
Mercurial honey
Violet honey
Rose honey
Powder of viper
Cornachine powder
Iacene powder
Diacartamy tablets
Agaric pills
Angle pills
Polireste salt
Soluble tartar
Mineral crystal
Emetic substance

Syrup of chicory
   combined with rhubarb
Soluble rose syrup
Syrup of flax
Syrup of Berbris
White poppy syrup
Laudanum
Balansts
Roses of Provins
Juice of licorice
Spirits of salt
Divinum
Bethonica
Diachilum
Devigo cum mercurio
Linen plasters
Contra fractu aram
Siccative
Mundatory
Suppurative
Apostolorum
Althea
Rose essence
Egyptiac
Fine turpentine
White wax
Pitch of Burgundy
Rose Oil
Worms

Puppy oil
Hypericum
Lily
Camomile
Oil of aspic
Balm of Peru
Aloe
Mastic
Myrrh
Dragon's blood
Sigillated earth
Colfil
Aristoloche
Guaiacum
Schine
Vitriol of sipre [?]
White vitriol
Alum érud
Corrosive sublimate
Red precipitate
Infernal stone
  [silver nitrate]
Cautery stone
Crochisque alby rhasis
Prepared sponge
Lancets
Syringes
Scissors
Scalpels

Canada. Public Archives. Manuscript Division, MG1, B, Vol. 15, pp. 118-21, Statement of necessary medical supplies to be procured from France for the troops in Canada, Versailles, 8 March 1688.

APPENDIX D

Imported Products as Advertised by John Minson Galt, Williamsburg, 1769

Crude antimony
Aether
Verdigrease
Barbados
Hepatick and succotrines aloes
Common and rock alum
Ambergrise
Compound waters of all kinds
Quick-silver
Balsams of capri, Peru, amber and Tolu
Canadian Balsams
Armenian bole
Borax
Calomel crude and prepared
Camphor
Canella alba
Cantharides
Cloves
Indian pink, greatly celebrated for destroying worms in children
Russian and Hudson's Bay castors
Common and lunar caustick
Cinnabar of antimony
Native and fictitious cinnabar
Potash
Cochineal
Colcothar
Vitriol
Colocynth
Confectio cardiaca
Conserves of hips
Sloes and sorrel roses
Worm-wood and orange peel
Jesuits bark
Cinnamon
Cascarilla
Cremor tartar
English and Spanish saffron

Claterium
Plaisters and electuaries of all kinds
Essence of lemons, burgamot and ambergrease
Single and double camomile flowers
Flower of brimstone
Balaustines
Senna
Galls
Grains of paradise
Gums of all kinds
Pearl barley
Isinglass
Irish flate
Litharge
Common and flakey manna
Sweet mercury
Calcined mercury
Corrosive sublimate
Red precipitate
Musk
Chymical oils
Opium
Long pepper
Ipecancuanha
Jalap
Gentian
Licorice
Contraverva
Calamus aromaticus
China and sarsaparilla
Best Turkey and Indian rhubarb
Valerian
Sago
Alkaline, neutral, and volatile salts
Saloop
Seeds of anise
Carraway coriander

Wild carrots
Fennel and fennugreek
Lesser cardamoms
Staves acre
Spermaceti
Spirits of hartshorn
Lavender
Sal volatile and sal ammoniac
Nitre
Mineral acids
Dulcified spirits of salt, vitriol, and salt ammoniac
Spanish licorice
Tartar emetic
Vermacelli
White, Blue, and green vitriols
Extract of hemlock
Glass of antimony
Meadows
Saffron
Mezeteon roots
Common and Nesbitt's clyster pipes
Gold and silver leaf
Dutch metal
Gallipots and vials
Anderson's, Hooper's and Lockyer's pills
Turlington's balsam
Hill's pectoral balsam of honey
Bateman's drops
Squire's, Daffy's and Bostock's elixirs
Freeman's and Godfrey's cordials
British oil
Eau de luce
Dr. James's fever powder
Court plaister
Best lavender and Hungary waters.

Thomas K. Ford, ed., *The Apothecary in Eighteenth-Century Williamsburg. Being an Account of His Medical and Chirurgical Services, as well as of his Trade Practices as a Chemist* (Williamsburg: Colonial Williamsburg, 1970), p. 24.

APPENDIX E

Selected Objects from Contexts Other Than That of the Stone Fort

The body of this study has not described objects from archaeological contexts other than that of the stone fort in the French period, yet some merit discussion. The artifacts are of particular interest because of their "typical" or common character, material used, evidence for a specific or seldom-represented function, etc.

The First Wooden Fort

29   Knife-saw (?)
This incomplete steel object consists of a flat, rectangular blade with bolsters and a central tang. One side of the blade has saw teeth; the other side is straight although its edge has apparently been eaten away by corrosion. (Photo by J. Jolin.)

30   Pioneer's sabre
Sabre blade and tang, with sawtooth back. This steel sabre could be used both as a weapon and as a saw for building wooden fortifications. (Photo by J. Jolin.)

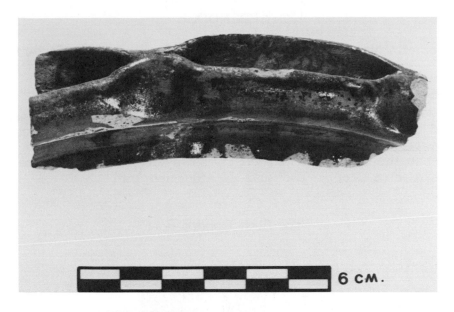

6 CM.

8 CM.

31 Large plate rim
The white fabric and green glaze of this ceramic piece reveal its French origin. The rim, which is particularly decorative, is split horizontally and pinched together at regular intervals. This form is known, but uncommon. (Photo by J. Jolin.)

32 Cooking pot fragment
Iron handle attached to a copper cooking pot. The right rivet is brass, the left rivet is copper. The handle would seem to be a replacement. (Photo by J. Jolin.)

33 Cooking pot fragment
Ear of a copper cooking pot, designed to receive the end of a handle. During the 17th century, copper and brass containers were extensively used for cooking. (Photo by J. Jolin.)

34 Jug or jar fragment
This fragment illustrates a material (coarse Rhenish stoneware) and a function (storage) that are both rather rare at Chambly. (Photo by J. Jolin.)

35 Glass fragment
Part of a container whose crizzled glass is typically French. Crizzling is due to impurities in the glass. (Photo by J. Jolin.)

36 Knee or garter buckle
Small decorated brass buckle that served to close knee breeches below the knee or tighten a garter. (Photo by J. Jolin.)

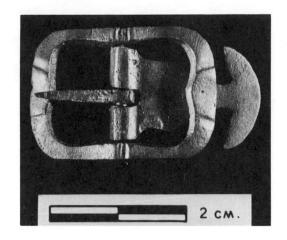

37 Coin
A copper Tours *double* bearing the portrait of Louis XIII was struck in 1642 (16G5G7-IQ). Because it came from the fort built in 1665, the coin must have been in use for at least 23 years after it was struck. The coin illustrated here (16G8K1-IQ), identical to the first coin, was found in a disturbed context. (Photo by N. Royer.)

38 Rosary bead
An oblong bead, probably ivory, decorated with horizontal carved lines. The identification of this object, while not absolutely certain, is highly plausible. If correctly identified, it would be the only object reflecting religious practices at Fort Chambly under the French régime. (Photo by J. Jolin.)

39 Table knife

This steel-bladed knife has a handle with bone scales, evidence of a certain luxury. The decoration of pointed circles was very possibly executed by the user (the lack of symmetry is particularly noteworthy). The design recalls certain slip-painted motifs of 18th-century Saintonge ceramic ware. (Photo by J. Jolin.)

The Fire Stratum

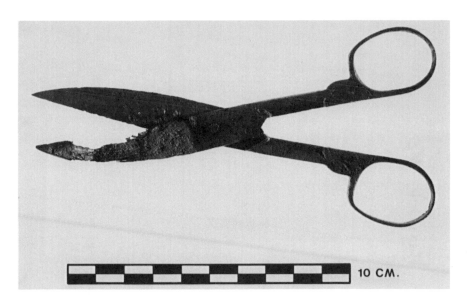

40 Scissors

These steel scissors, which may have been used to cut cloth or other materials, have identical flat, oval loops and semi-elliptical blades. (Photo by J. Jolin.)

41 Wood chisel

A complete tool, apparently of steel. It was forged from a square metal rod that was flattened into a cutting edge at one end and flared at the other to form a head. (Photo by J. Jolin.)

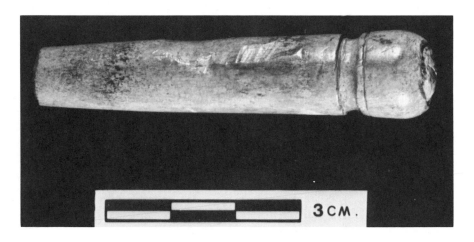

42 Handle

Bone handle of an undetermined type of tool, perhaps an awl. The unsophisticated, rather crude execution suggests that this item was made by an occupant of the fort. (Photo by J. Jolin.)

43 Sword

Blade and tang of a steel sword. This is a fairly typical model. The overall shape is triangular, and in section it forms an elongated diamond. (Photo by J. Jolin.)

44 Knife blade and tang
The size and sturdiness of this steel knife suggests that it was used for preparing food rather than for eating. (Photo by J. Jolin.)

45 Egg cup
This tin-glazed earthenware object is rare because of its green glaze. Its presence at Fort Chambly is all the more unusual in that its function suggests a rather studied refinement. (Photo by J. Jolin.)

46 Sole
The leather of this sole is smooth on one side and rough on the other. A groove and series of needle marks follow the contour of the foot, and the heel is pierced with several small holes. Its small size (19.7 cm by 7.4 cm) suggests that it belonged to a woman's or child's shoe. (Photo by J. Jolin.)

47 Tinkling cones
The copper ornaments were trade goods used in the fur trade. (Photo by J. Jolin.)

48 Gambling die
This is the only item representing games of chance, which were very popular. The numbers on this bone die have been marked with a drill. (Photo by J. Jolin.)

49 Officer's pike
This iron point has a socket on one end that is designed to fit over a wooden shaft. The pike, a descendant of the lances of the Middle Ages, was a mark of distinction for its bearer. (Photo by J. Jolin.)

50 Axe-head
Axe 16G8P6-1Q, made of iron and steel and ending in a pick, must have been a ship's boarding axe or a trading axe. A similar axe (16G5G17-1Q) is shown here. (Photo by J. Jolin.)

51 Sword handle

This sword handle, made of moulded brass, is representative of the model supplied to soldiers. (Photo by J. Jolin.)

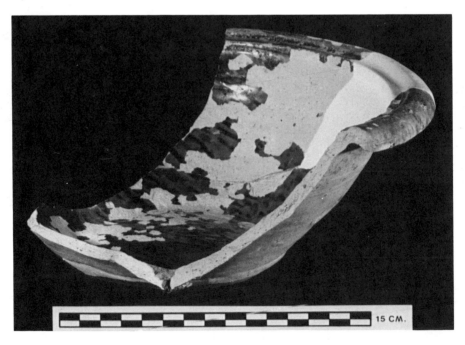

52 Large dish

Large coarse earthenware dish. This piece, reconstructable, gives us a good idea of the kind of imported French dishes that were used for mixing, settling or separating (e.g., milk and cream), and other purposes. The buff-coloured fabric and green glaze are typical of French ceramics. (Photo by J. Jolin.)

53 Sword hilt

All that remains is the lower part of the hilt (ricasso, hand guard, remains of collar, and stub of connecting arc). The hilt is made of unusual materials. The collar, to judge from its remains, consisted of one (or perhaps two) sheets of copper covered with iron on both sides. The reason for this metallurgical procedure has not yet been explained. The rest of the sword seems to be made entirely of iron. The ricasso is decorated with stamped rectangles, and the cross-piece ends in a large drop. The hand guard and connecting arc are decorated with a helical groove. (Photo by J. Jolin.)

54 Plate fragment

A coarse French earthenware plate is shallow, covered with slip on the inside, and decorated on the brim with slip-painted zig-zag motifs. (Photo by J. Jolin.)

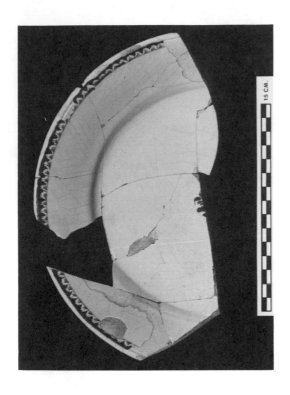

55 Plate (reconstructable)
Shallow tin-glazed plate with broad
brim. Executed in the French style
of Rouen, it is decorated with Chinese motifs adapted by Guillibaud. It
would appear to date from the second quarter of the 18th century
(Genêt 1980: 33, Fig. 13b). The blue
rim band has a resist design of
crude, outlined palmettes with clus-
ters of small lines. The centre of
the plate has a small, outlined floral
motif. (Photo by J. Jolin.)

56 Plate (reconstructable)
Shallow tin-glazed plate with narrow brim. It is Dutch and apparently dates from the end of the 17th
century or the beginning of the 18th
(Genêt 1980: 60, Pl. 89d). The brim
is decorated with concentric ovals
and plant motifs (acorns and foliated scrolls); the bottom has two
concentric circles surrounding a
basket of stylized fruit (or flowers).
(Photo by J. Jolin.)

NOTES

Introduction

1 Cyrille Gélinas, "Le rôle du fort de Chambly dans le développement de la Nouvelle-France, 1665-1760," Travail inédit No. 392, Parks Canada, Ottawa, 1977, p. 119.

2 Jean Hamelin et al., Histoire du Québec (St-Hyacinthe: Edisem, 1977), p. 250.

Part One: The Geographical, Historical, and Social Contexts

1 Cyrille Gélinas, op. cit., pp. 4-8.

2 This succession of events is deliberately schematic. For a complete picture of the political context of this period, and in particular of the role of Louis XIV, see Jacques Mathieu's "Province de France" in Jean Hamelin, op. cit., pp. 127-82, from which my facts have been taken.

3 Louise Dechêne, Habitants et marchands de Montréal au XVIIe siècle (Paris: Plon, 1974), p. 386.

4 Cyrille Gélinas and Michelle Guitard-Fortin, "Fort Chambly. Dossier structural. Régime français et régime anglais," manuscript on file, Historical and Archaeological Research, Quebec Regional Office, Environment Canada — Parks, Quebec, 1979, pp. 22-23.

5 Gisèle Piédalue, pers. com., 1982.

6 Cyrille Gélinas and Michelle Guitard-Fortin, op. cit., p. 5.

7 Gisèle Piédalue, pers. com., 1982.

8 Jean-François Blanchette, "L'importance des artefacts dans l'étude des modes d'alimentation en Nouvelle-France," Histoire et archéologie, No. 52 (1981), p. 64.

9 François Miville-Deschênes and Gisèle Piédalue, "Étude binaire. L'origine des céramiques et la quincaillerie architecturale au fort Chambly," Travail inédit No. 433, Parks Canada, Ottawa, 1980, pp. 7-8.

10 Cyrille Gélinas, op. cit., p. 70.

11 For the history of the fort, see Cyrille Gélinas, op. cit.

12 Cyrille Gélinas, op. cit., p. 141.

13 Gilles Proulx, "Soldat à Québec, 1748-1759," Travail inédit No. 242, Parks Canada, Ottawa, 1977 (hereafter cited as "Soldat"), p. 100.

14 Canada. Public Archives. Manuscript Division (hereafter cited as PAC), MG2, C^7, carton 40.

15 Jacques Mathieu in Jean Hamelin et al., op. cit., pp. 183-230.

16 Jean Hamelin et al., op. cit., p. 209.

17 Ibid., p. 227.

18 Pierre Nadon, "Fort Chambly: A Narrative History," Manuscript Report Series No. 75, Parks Canada, Ottawa, 1965, p. 20.

19 Cyrille Gélinas, op. cit., pp. 122-23.

20 Ibid., p. 123.

21 Pierre Nadon, op. cit., p. 25.

22 Cyrille Gélinas, op. cit., pp. 123-24.

23 Ibid., p. 124.

24 Ibid., p. 125.

25 Quebec (Prov.). Archives nationales (Montréal) (hereafter cited as ANQM), Greffe G. Barette, marriage contract between Pierre Pépin dit Laforce ... and Michelle Leber, Laprairie, 30 Nov. 1714.

26 France. Archives nationales. Archives des colonies (hereafter cited as AC), $C^{11}A$, Vol. 119, fols. 71, 450.

27 Dictionnaire biographique du Canada (Quebec: Presses de l'université Laval, 1966-), Vol. 4, s.v. "Antoine Grisé."

28 Cyrille Gélinas, op. cit., p. 127.

29 François Miville-Deschênes and Gisèle Piédalue, op. cit., pp. 111-12.

30 ANQM, Archives judiciaires (hereafter cited as AJ), the king vs Sansquartier, Lajeunesse and Langevin, various documents, 5-7 Feb. 1719.

31 Gilles Proulx, "Soldat," p. 25.

32 Ibid., pp. 25-26.

33 Ibid., pp. 26-27.

34 Ibid., p. 6.
35 Ibid., p. 20.
36 Cyrille Gélinas, op. cit., pp. 35-37.
37 W. J.Eccles, "The Social, Economic, and Political Significance of the Military Establishment in New-France," Canadian Historical Review, Vol. 52, No. 1 (March 1971), p. 6.
38 Cyrille Gélinas, pers. com., 1981.
39 Ibid.
40 Cameron Nish, Les bourgeois-gentilshommes de la Nouvelle-France, 1729-1748 (Montreal: Fides, 1968), p. 78.
41 Ibid., p. 83.
42 Ibid., p. 78.
43 Pierre Nadon, op. cit., p. 56.
44 Cameron Nish, op. cit., p. 179.
45 Ibid.
46 Louis Franquet, Voyages et mémoires sur le Canada (Montreal: Éditions Élysée, 1974), p. 88.
47 ANQM, Greffe A. Adhémar, marriage contract between Jean Marllaut and Roberde Péladeau, Fort St-Louis, 11 June 1690; Greffe G. Hodresne, marriage contract between Jacques Gagnon and Marianne Vergette dit Prénoveau, 26 Oct. 1741; Greffe D. De Blazy, marriage contract between Pierre François Macabée and Marie Catherine Simon, Montreal, 5 Jan. 1758.
48 AC, C11A, Vol. 11, p. 289, Champigny to minister, 12 Oct. 1691.
49 Ibid., Vol. 47, fols. 73, 78v, Longueuil and Bégon to minister, 31 Oct. 1725; B, Vol. 50, fol. 488, minister to Beauharnois, 12 April 1727.

Part Two: Domestic Life in the Stone Fort (1709-1760)

1 Lyle M. Stone, Fort Michilimackinac, 1715-1781. An Archeological Perspective on the Revolutionary Frontier (East Lansing: Michigan State University, 1974), p. 354.
2 Guy Chaussinand-Nogaret, La vie quotidienne des Français sous Louis XV (Paris: Hachette, 1979), pp. 37-38.
3 AC, C11A, Vol. 62, fols. 34, 35v, Hocquart to minister, 10 Oct. 1734.
4 ANQM, Greffe P. Panet, contract between Langevin and Louis Pinusseault, Montreal, 4 Dec. 1758.
5 AC, C11A, Vol. 114, fols. 109, 280v-284.
6 Cyrille Gélinas, op. cit., p. 135.
7 AC, C11A, Vol. 113-2, fol. 314; Vol. 162, fol. 63v; Vol. 70, fol. 74v.
8 Ibid., Vol. 55, fol. 274; Vol. 60, fol. 229v; Vol. 113-2, fol. 442.
9 Jean Vidalenc, La petite métallurgie rurale en Haute Normandie sous l'ancien régime (Paris: Éditions Domat-Montchrestien, 1946), pp. 93-102.
10 Gilles Proulx, "Soldat," p. 104.
11 Ibid., p. 102.
12 AC, C11A, Vol. 119, fols. 03-09.
13 Gisèle Piédalue, pers. com., 1982.
14 Peter N. Moogk, Building a House in New-France. An Account of the Perplexities of Client and Craftsmen in Early Canada ([Toronto]: McClelland and Stewart, [1975]), pp. 38-45.
15 Ivor Noël Hume, A Guide to Artifacts of Colonial America (New York: Alfred A. Knopf, 1976), p. 233.
16 AC, C11A, Vol. 60, fol. 236v; Vol. 70, fol. 74v; Vol. 79, fol. 382v; Vol. 81, fol. 489; Vol. 114, fols. 54, 284, 379v, 1182; Vol. 115, fols. 104, 106.
17 Ibid., Vol. 47, fols. 73, 78v; Vol. 18, fols. 157-158, 31 Oct. 1725.
18 Gilles Proulx, "Soldat," p. 77.
19 AC, C11A, Vol. 55, fol. 274; Cyrille Gélinas, pers. com., 1981.
20 ANQM, AJ, the king vs Sansquartier, Lajeunesse and Langevin, Information, 6 Feb. 1719.
21 Marcel Moussette, "Le chauffage domestique en Nouvelle-France, 1729-1748," Travail inédit No. 75, Parks Canada, Ottawa, 1971, pp. 101-103.
22 Ibid., pp. 78-80.
23 AC, C11A, Vol. 55, fol. 274; Vol. 60, fol. 229v.
24 Nora Dawson, La vie traditionnelle à Saint-Pierre (île d'Orleans) (Quebec: Presses de l'université Laval, 1960), p. 31.
25 Henri-Raymond Casgrain, ed., Col-

lection de manuscrits du maréchal de Lévis (Quebec: Demers et frère, 1891), Vol. 5, p. 80.

26 Marcel Moussette, op. cit., pp. 78-80.
27 Ibid., p. 88.
28 Robert-Lionel Séguin, La civilisation traditionnelle de l' "habitant" aux XVIIe et XVIIIe siècles (Montreal: Fides, 1973) (hereafter cited as Civilisation), p. 345.
29 Arthur H. Hayward, Colonial and Early American Lighting (New York: Dover Publications, 1962), p. 3.
30 Robert-Lionel Séguin, Civilisation, p. 345.
31 Arthur H. Hayward, op. cit., p. 11.
32 Robert-Lionel Séguin, Civilisation, p. 345.
33 AC, C11A, Vol. 114, fols. 98-355, 280v-284.
34 Ibid., Vol. 119, fols. 03-09.
35 Robert-Lionel Séguin, Civilisation, p. 345.
36 AC, C11A, Vol. 114, fols. 280v-284v.
37 Robert-Lionel Séguin, Civilisation, p. 346.
38 AC, C11A, Vol. 114, fols. 351-55.
39 Gilles Proulx, "Soldat," pp. 76-78.
40 AC, C11A, Vol. 113-2, fol. 442; Vol. 55, fol. 274; Vol. 60, fol. 229v.
41 Ibid., Vol. 113-2, fol. 442; Vol. 60, fol. 229v; Vol. 55, fol. 274.
42 Louise Dechêne, op. cit., p. 386.
43 PAC, MG2, B1, Vol. 42, fol. 21.
44 Cyrille Gélinas, pers. com., 1982.
45 Allan Greer, "Les soldats de l'Île Royale, 1720-1745," Histoire et archéologie, No. 28 (1979), pp. 38-42.
46 Pehr Kalm, Voyage de Pehr Kalm au Canada en 1749, trans. and annotated by Jacques Rousseau and Guy Béthune ([Montreal]: Cercle du Livre de France, 1977), p. 126.
47 Gilles Proulx, "Soldat," p. 91.
48 Louis Franquet, op. cit., p. 86.
49 Kent G. Walker and Stephen L. Cumbaa, "Life on the Frontier, 1665-1760: A Zooarchaeological Look at Fort Chambly, Quebec," manuscript on file, Zooarchaeological Identification Centre, National Museum of Natural Sciences, Ottawa, 1982, p. 74.
50 AC, C11A, Vol. 35, fol. 180.
51 Pehr Kalm, op. cit., pp. 126, 573.
52 Jean-François Blanchette, op. cit.
53 Kent G. Walker and Stephen L. Cumbaa, op. cit., pp. 68-69.
54 H. R. Casgrain, ed., op. cit., p. 233.
55 Kent G. Walker and Stephen L. Cumbaa, op. cit., p. 67.
56 Pehr Kalm, op. cit., p. 84.
57 AC, C11A, Vol. 70, fols. 67-68v.
58 Robert-Lionel Séguin, Civilisation, pp. 438-39.
59 Pehr Kalm, op. cit., pp. 129-30.
60 The origins of this ceramic ware will not be examined in detail here because it has been the subject of a previous study, see François Miville-Deschênes and Gisèle Piédalue, op. cit.
61 Jean-François Blanchette, op. cit., p. 31.
62 Kent G. Walker and Stephen L. Cumbaa, op. cit., p. 65.
63 Ibid., pp. 33, 61, 66.
64 Ibid., p. 61.
65 Suzanne Tardieu, La vie domestique dans le mâconnais rural préindustriel (Paris: Institut d'ethnologie, 1964), pp. 109-112.
66 Kenneth James Barton, "Terres cuites grossières provenant de la forteresse de Louisbourg," Histoire et archéologie, No. 55 (1981), p. 22.
67 Jean-François Blanchette, op. cit., p. 52.
68 Ibid., p. 30.
69 Ibid., pp. 34-35.
70 Frances Phipps, Colonial Kitchens, their Furnishings and their Gardens (New York: Hawthorn Books, 1972), p. 88.
71 AC, C11A, Vol. 119, fols. 03-09.
72 Robert-Lionel Séguin, Les ustensiles en Nouvelle-France (Montreal: Leméac, 1972) (hereafter cited as Ustensiles), p. 42.
73 Luce Vermette, "La vie domestique aux Forges du Saint-Maurice," Travail inédit No. 274, Parks Canada, Ottawa, 1977, pp. 93-94.
74 Frances Phipps, op. cit., pp. 83-84.
75 AC, F3, Vol. 9, fol. 372.

76 Marcel Trudel, Initiation à la Nouvelle-France. Histoire et institutions (Montreal: Holt, Rinehart and Winston, 1968), p. 212.

77 AC, Vol. 40, fols. 457v, 458, minister to Vaudreuil and Bégon, 5 April 1718.

78 François Miville-Deschênes and Gisèle Piédalue, op. cit., p. 21.

79 Olive Jones, pers. com., 1982.

80 Marcel Trudel, op. cit., p. 212.

81 Jean Elisabeth Lunn, "The Illegal Fur Trade out of New-France, 1713-1760," Canadian Historical Association Report (1939), p. 63.

82 Ibid., p. 61.

83 Pierre-Georges Roy, Ordonnances des intendants (Beauceville: L'Éclaireur, 1919), Vol. 1, p. 249.

84 AC, B, Vol. 57, fol. 674, minister to Beauharnois and Hocquart, 22 April 1732.

85 Jean Elisabeth Lunn, op. cit., p. 68.

86 Ibid., p. 63.

87 Ivor Noël Hume, op. cit., p. 115.

88 Ibid.

89 Lyle M. Stone, op. cit., pp. 169-70.

90 Ivor Noël Hume, op. cit., p. 117.

91 Gérard Gusset, "Inventaire général des grès blancs fins à glaçure saline," Histoire et archéologie, No. 38 (1980), pp. 93-95.

92 Ibid., p. 91.

93 Ibid., p. 9.

94 Nicole Genêt, Les collections archéologiques de la place Royale. La faïence (Quebec: Ministère des Affaires culturelles, Direction générale du patrimoine, 1980), pp. 52, 49.

95 Gilles Proulx, "A la défense de la Nouvelle-France," manuscript on file, Historical and Archaeological Research, Quebec Regional Office, Environment Canada — Parks, Quebec, 1981 (hereafter cited as "Défense"), p. 72.

96 Jean Federico Taylor, "Eighteenth-Century Ceramics at the DAR Museum," Antiques (April 1978), p. 840.

97 Nicole Genêt, op cit., p. 50.

98 Ivor Noël Hume, op. cit., p. 136.

99 François Miville-Deschênes and Gisèle Piédalue, op. cit., p. 130.

100 Hélène Deslauriers, pers. com., 1977.

101 Ivor Noël Hume, op. cit., p. 191.

102 Jane E. Harris, "Articles de verre mis au jour à Beaubassin, Nouvelle-Écosse," Lieux historiques canadiens: cahiers d'archéologie et d'histoire, No. 13 (1980), p. 141.

103 Ivor Noël Hume, op. cit., pp. 195-96.

104 Olive Jones, pers. com., 1982.

105 L.M. Bickerton, An Illustrated Guide to Eighteenth-Century English Drinking Glasses (London: Barrie and Jenkins, 1971), p. 304.

106 François Miville-Deschênes and Gisèle Piédalue, op. cit., p. 23.

107 J. Jefferson Miller and Lyle M. Stone, Eighteenth-Century Ceramics from Fort Michilimackinac; A Study in Historical Archeology (Washington, D.C.: Smithsonian Institution Press, 1970), p. 90.

108 Ivor Noël Hume, op. cit., p. 257.

109 Robert-Lionel Séguin, Civilisation, p. 381.

110 J. Jefferson Miller and Lyle M. Stone, op. cit., p. 81.

111 Ibid.

112 Robert-Lionel Séguin, Civilisation, p. 381.

113 Simon Courcy, pers. com., 1981.

114 Robert-Lionel Séguin, Civilisation, p. 522.

115 Jacques Mathieu, Le commerce entre la Nouvelle-France et les Antilles au XVIIIe siècle (Montreal: Fides, 1981), pp. 170-171.

116 Ivor Noël Hume, op. cit.; J. Jefferson Miller and Lyle M. Stone, op. cit.

117 J. Jefferson Miller and Lyle M. Stone, op. cit., p. 86.

118 Kenneth James Barton, "Les terres cuites grossières de l'Europe occidentale livrées par l'épave du Machault," Lieux historiques canadiens: cahiers d'archéologie et d'histoire, No. 16 (1978), (hereafter cited as Machault), p. 67.

119 Gérard Gusset, op. cit., p. 9.

120 Louis Franquet, op. cit., p. 88.

121 Barbara J. Wade, "Cutlery from the Roma Site, Brudenell Point, Prince Edward Island," manuscript on file,

Environment Canada — Parks, Ottawa, 1975, p. 22.

122 Nicole Genêt, op. cit., Pl. 46.

123 Jean-François Blanchette, op. cit., p. 49, Fig. 4.

124 Albert Barbeau, Les bourgeois d'autrefois (Paris: Firmin-Didot, 1886), p. 203.

125 Jean-François Blanchette, op. cit., pp. 49-50.

126 Nicole Genêt, op. cit., Fig. 16.

127 Idem, op.cit..

128 Gilles Proulx, "Défense," p. 73.

129 Kenneth James Barton, Machault, p. 66.

130 Louise Bernard, pers. com., 1982.

131 Nicole Genêt, Luce Vermette and Louise Décarie-Audet, Les objets familiers de nos ancêtres (Montreal: Éditions de l'Homme, 1974), pp. 95-97.

132 Robert-Lionel Séguin, Ustensiles, p. 2.

133 Louise Bernard, "Les cuillères d'étain du Québec," MA thesis, Université Laval, Quebec, 1978, pp. 28-29.

134 Luce Vermette, op. cit., p. 96.

135 Frances Phipps, op. cit., p. 82.

136 AC, C^{11}A, Vol. 119, fols. 03-09.

137 Ibid., Vol. 114, fol. 280v.

138 Nicole Genêt, Luce Vermette and Louise Décarie-Audet, op. cit., p. 58.

139 Ibid., p. 57.

140 Ibid.

141 Jacques Mathieu, op cit.

142 Nicole Genêt, Luce Vermette and Louise Décarie-Audet, op. cit., p. 56.

143 Robert-Lionel Séguin, Civilisation, pp. 523-25.

144 Gilles Proulx, "Soldat," p. 93.

145 Jean-François Blanchette, op. cit., p. 73.

146 Luce Vermette, op. cit., p. 120.

147 PAC, MG1, C^{11}A, Vol. 99, pp. 68-73, Duquesne to minister, Quebec, 26 Oct. 1753.

148 Gilles Proulx, "Soldat," p. 77.

149 ANQM, AJ, the king vs Jacques Bonin dit Laforest, sergeant in the Compagnie d'Esgly, 19 Feb. 1716.

150 ANQM, Greffe G. de Chèvremont, "Inventaire des biens de la succession de Joseph Déjourdy sieur de Cabanac, lieutenant," 27 March 1737.

151 A surgeon was present in 1719, 1720, 1727, 1728, 1729, 1732, 1734, 1736, 1737, 1738, 1739, 1740, 1741, 1742, 1748, and 1760. Cyrille Gélinas, pers. com., 1981.

152 Guy Chaussinand-Nogaret, op. cit., p. 172.

153 Ibid., p. 173.

154 ANQM, AJ, the king vs Sansquartier, Lajeunesse, and Langevin, declaration Charles Carpentier, 5 Feb. 1719.

155 AC, C^{11}A, Vol. 70, fol. 84; Vol. 79, fol. 407; Vol. 114, fols. 39v, 117, 288.

156 Yvon Desloges, pers. com., 1982.

157 Thomas K. Ford, ed., The Apothecary in Eighteenth-Century Williamsburg. Being an Account of his Medical and Chirurgical Services, as well as of his Trade Practices as a Chemist (Williamsburg: Colonial Williamsburg, 1970), p. 23.

158 Gilles Proulx, "Soldat," p. 50.

159 Marcel Trudel, op. cit., p. 241.

160 Gilles Proulx, "Soldat," p. 102.

161 AC, C^{11}A. Vol. 117, fol. 250v; Vol. 116, fol. 250v; Vol. 117-1, p. 37.

162 Gilles Proulx, "Soldat," p. 105.

163 Ibid., p. 103.

164 Lyle M. Stone, op. cit., p. 53.

165 Edward P. Hamilton, L'armée française en Amérique (Ottawa: Museum Restoration Services, 1967), p. 6.

166 René Chartrand, pers. com., 1980.

167 Pehr Kalm, op. cit., p. 183.

168 Luce Vermette, op. cit., pp. 110-13.

169 Robert-Lionel Séguin, Civilisation, p. 459.

170 Cyrille Gélinas, pers. com., 1982.

171 PAC, MG23, G5, 7, carton 10, fol. 127, Jonquière to de Muy, 25 June 1751.

172 PAC, MG1, C^{11}A, Vol. 99, p. 69, Duquesne to minister, 26 Oct. 1753.

173 Iain C. Walker, "Étude archéologique des pipes en terre provenant du bastion du Roi à la forteresse de Louisbourg," Lieux historiques canadiens: cahiers d'archéologie et

d'histoire, No. 2 (1974), p. 89.

174 Ibid., p. 99, Fig. 30.

175 Lyle M. Stone, op. cit., p. 148, Figs. 78-J, 150.

176 Gilles Proulx, "Soldat," p. lll.

177 Iain C. Walker, op. cit., pp. 45-46.

178 Robert-Lionel Séguin, Civilisation, pp. 193-96.

179 Cyrille Gélinas, "Réflexions préliminaires à une étude de la vallée du Richelieu; quelques observations générales sur trois siècles d'agriculture et d'exploitation forestière," Travail inédit No. 414, Parks Canada, Ottawa, 1980, p. 31.

180 Robert-Lionel Séguin, Les divertissements en Nouvelle-France, Ottawa: National Museum of Canada, 1968, p. 54.

181 ANQM, AJ, "Meurtre ... de Laviolette ... par le Provencal," 5 May 1722.

182 Charles Kunstler, La vie quotidienne sous la Régence (Paris: Hachette, 1960), p. 196.

183 Lyle M. Stone, op. cit., p. 154.

REFERENCES CITED

Barbeau, Albert
Les bourgeois d'autrefois. Firmin-Didot, Paris, 1886.

Barton, Kenneth James
"Les terres cuites grossières de l'Europe occidentale livrées par l'épave du Machault." Lieux historiques canadiens: cahiers d'archéologie et d'histoire, No. 16 (1978), pp. 45-72. Ottawa. (Published in English as "The Western European Coarse Earthenwares from the Wreck of the Machault," Canadian Historic Sites: Occasional Papers in Archaeology and History, No. 16 1977 , pp. 45-71, Ottawa.)
"Terres cuites grossières provenant de la forteresse de Louisbourg." Histoire et archéologie, No. 55 (1981), pp. 3-78. Ottawa. (Published in English as "Coarse Earthenwares from the Fortress of Louisbourg," History and Archaeology, No. 55 [1981], pp. 3-74, Ottawa.)

Bernard, Louise
"Les cuillères d'étain du Québec." MA thesis, Université Laval, Quebec, 1978.

Bickerton, L.M.
An Illustrated Guide to Eighteenth-Century English Drinking Glasses. Barrie and Jenkins, London, 1971.

Blanchette, Jean-François
"L'importance des artefacts dans l'étude des modes d'alimentation en Nouvelle-France." Histoire et archéologie, No. 52 (1981). Ottawa. (Published in English as "The Role of Artifacts in the Study of Foodways in New France, 1720-1760," History and Archaeology, No. 52 [1981], Ottawa.)

Canada. Department of the Environment. Parks. Quebec Regional Office. Historical and Archaeological Research. Material Culture Research Group.
"Matériaux des objets: répertoire de mots-clés." Manuscript on file, Quebec, 1981.

"Techniques, fonctions et usages des objets: répertoire de mots-clés." Manuscript on file, Quebec, 1978.

Canada. Public Archives. Manuscript Division.
MG1, B, Lettres envoyées.
MG1, $C^{11}A$, Correspondance générale, Canada.
MG2, B^1, Décisions, Délibérations du Conseil de Marine, 1715-1721.
MG2, C^7, Personnel individuel.
MG23, G5, 7, Quebec and Lower Canada, Miscellaneous, Hospice-Anthelme-Jean-Baptiste Verreau.

Casgrain, Henri-Raymond, ed.
Collection de manuscrits du maréchal de Lévis. Demers et frère, Quebec, 1891. 12 vols.

Chaussinand-Nogaret, Guy
La vie quotidienne des Français sous Louis XV. Hachette, Paris, 1979.

Dawson, Nora
La vie traditionnelle à Saint-Pierre (île d'Orléans). Presses de l'université Laval, Quebec, 1960. Les archives de folklore, No. 8.

Dechêne, Louise
Habitants et marchands de Montréal au XVIIe siècle. Plon, Paris, 1974.

Dictionnaire biographique du Canada
Presses de l'université Laval, Quebec, 1966-, Vol. 4: 1771-1800.

Eccles, W.J.
"The Social, Economic, and Political Significance of the Military Establishment in New-France." Canadian Historical Review, Vol. 52, No. 1 (March 1971), pp. 1-22.

Ford, Thomas K., ed.
The Apothecary in Eighteenth-Century Williamsburg. Being an Account of his

Medical and Chirurgical Services, as well as of his Trade Practices as a Chemist. Colonial Williamsburg, Williamsburg, 1970.

France. Archives nationales. Archives des colonies.
B, Lettres envoyées.
C^{11}A, Correspondance générale.
F^3, Collection Moreau de Saint-Méry.

Franquet, Louis
Voyages et mémoires sur le Canada. Rev. ed. Éditions Élysée, Montreal, 1974.

Gélinas, Cyrille
"Le rôle du fort de Chambly dans le développement de la Nouvelle-France, 1665-1760." Travail inédit No. 392, Parks Canada, Ottawa, 1977. (The copy I used included unpublished corrections made by the author. The revised work has been published as The Role of Fort Chambly in the Development of New France, 1665-1760, Parks Canada, Ottawa, 1983, [Studies in Archaeology, Architecture and History].)
"Réflexions préliminaires à une étude de la vallée du Richelieu; quelques observations générales sur trois siècles d'agriculture et d'exploitation forestière." Travail inédit No. 414, Parks Canada, Ottawa, 1980.

Gélinas, Cyrille, and Michelle Guitard-Fortin
"Fort Chambly. Dossier structural. Régime français et régime anglais." Manuscript on file, Historical and Archaeological Research, Quebec Regional Office, Environment Canada — Parks, Quebec, 1979.

Genêt, Nicole
Les collections archéologiques de la place Royale. La faïence. Ministère des Affaires culturelles, Direction générale du patrimoine, Quebec, 1980. Dossier 45.

Genêt, Nicole, Luce Vermette and Louise Décarie-Audet
Les objets familiers de nos ancêtres. Preface by Robert-Lionel Séguin. Éditions de l'Homme, Montreal, 1974.

Greer, Allan
"Les soldats de l'Île Royale, 1720-1745." Histoire et archéologie, No. 28 (1979). Ottawa. (Published in English as "The Soldiers of Isle Royale, 1720-45," History and Archaeology, No. 28 [1979], Ottawa.)

Gusset, Gérard
"Inventaire général des grès blancs fins à glaçure saline." Histoire et archéologie, No. 38 (1980). Ottawa. (Published in English as "Stoneware: White Salt-glazed, Rhenish and Dry Body," History and Archaeology, No. 38 [1980], Ottawa.)

Hamelin, Jean, et al.
Histoire du Québec. Edisem, St-Hyacinthe, 1977.

Hamilton, Edward P.
L'armée française en Amérique. Museum Restoration Services, Ottawa, 1967.

Harris, Jane E.
"Articles de verre mis au jour à Beaubassin, Nouvelle-Écosse." Lieux historiques canadiens: cahiers d'archéologie et d'histoire, No. 13 (1980), pp. 129-45. Ottawa. (Published in English as "Glassware Excavated at Beaubassin, Nova Scotia," Canadian Historic Sites: Occasional Papers in Archaeology and History, No. 13 [1975], pp. 127-42, Ottawa.)

Hayward, Arthur H.
Colonial and Early American Lighting. 3rd ed. Dover Publications, New York, 1962.

Kalm, Pehr
Voyage de Pehr Kalm au Canada en 1749. Trans. and annotated by Jacques Rousseau and Guy Béthune. Cercle du Livre de France, [Montreal], 1977.

Kunstler, Charles
La vie quotidienne sous la Régence. Hachette, Paris, 1960.

Lunn, Jean Elisabeth
"The Illegal Fur Trade out of New-France, 1713-1760." Canadian Historical Association Report, 1939, pp. 61-79.

Mathieu, Jacques
Le commerce entre la Nouvelle-France et les Antilles au XVIIIe siècle. Fides, Montreal, 1981.

Miller, J. Jefferson, and Lyle M. Stone
Eighteenth-Century Ceramics from Fort Michilimackinac; A Study in Historical Archeology. Smithsonian Institution Press, Washington, D.C., 1970. Smithsonian Studies in History and Technology, No. 4.

Miville-Deschênes, François, and Gisèle Piédalue
"Étude binaire. L'origine des céramiques et la quincaillerie architecturale au fort Chambly." Travail inédit No. 433, Parks Canada, Ottawa, 1980.

Moogk, Peter N.
Building a House in New-France. An Account of the Perplexities of Client and Craftsmen in Early Canada. McClelland and Stewart, [Toronto, 1975].

Moussette, Marcel
"Le chauffage domestique en Nouvelle-France." Travail inédit No. 75, Parks Canada, Ottawa, 1971.

Nadon, Pierre
"Fort Chambly: A Narrative History." Manuscript Report Series No. 17, Parks Canada, Ottawa, 1965.

Nish, Cameron
Les bourgeois-gentilshommes de la Nouvelle-France, 1729-1748. Fides, Montreal, 1968.

Noël Hume, Ivor
A Guide to Artifacts of Colonial America. Alfred A. Knopf, New York, 1976.

Phipps, Frances
Colonial Kitchens, their Furnishings and their Gardens. Hawthorn Books, New York, 1972.

Proulx, Gilles
"A la défense de la Nouvelle-France." Manuscript on file, Historical and Archaeological Research, Quebec Regional Office, Environment Canada — Parks, Quebec, 1981. (Now printed in the series Travail inédit, No. 435).
"Soldat à Québec, 1748-1759." Travail inédit No. 242, Parks Canada, Ottawa, 1977.

Quebec (Prov.). Archives nationales (Montreal).
Greffes des notaires.
Archives judiciaires.

Roy, Pierre-Georges
Ordonnances des intendants. L'Éclaireur, Beauceville, 1919. 4 vols.

Séguin, Robert-Lionel
La civilisation traditionnelle de l' "habitant" aux XVIIe et XVIIIe siècles. 2nd ed. rev. Fides, Montreal, 1973.
Les divertissements en Nouvelle-France. National Museum of Canada, Ottawa, 1968. Bulletin No. 227.
Les ustensiles en Nouvelle-France. Léméac, Montreal, 1972.

Stone, Lyle M.
Fort Michilimackinac, 1715-1781. An Archeological Perspective on the Revolutionary Frontier. Michigan State University, East Lansing, 1974. Publications of the Museum, Anthropological Series, Vol. 2.

Tardieu, Suzanne
La vie domestique dans le mâconnais rural préindustriel. Institut d'ethnologie, Paris, 1964.

Taylor, Jean Federico
"Eighteenth-Century Ceramics at the DAR Museum." Antiques (April 1978), pp. 838-48.

Trudel, Marcel
Initiation à la Nouvelle-France. Histoire et institutions. Holt, Rinehart and Winston, Montreal, 1968.

Vermette, Luce
"La vie domestique aux Forges du Saint-Maurice." Travail inédit No. 274, Parks Canada, Ottawa, 1977. (Now published in English as "Domestic Life at Les Forges

du Saint-Maurice," History and Archaeology, No. 58 [1982], Ottawa.)

Veyrier, Henri
Dictionnaire des jeux. Éditions Princesse, n.p., n.d.

Vidalenc, Jean
La petite métallurgie rurale en Haute Normandie sous l'ancien régime. Éditions Domat-Montchrestien, Paris, 1946.

Wade, Barbara J.
"Cutlery from the Roma Site, Brudenell Point, Prince Edward Island." Manuscript on file, National Historic Parks and Sites Branch, Environment Canada — Parks, Ottawa, 1975. (Now published in History and Archaeology, No. 27 [1979], pp. 105-38, Ottawa.)

Walker, Iain C.
"Clay Tobacco-Pipes, with Particular Reference to the Bristol Industry." History and Archaeology, No. 11 (1977). Ottawa.
"Étude archéologique des pipes en terre provenant du bastion du Roi à la forteresse de Louisbourg," Lieux historiques canadiens: cahiers d'archéologie et d'histoire, No. 2 (1974), pp. 60-128. Ottawa. (Published in English as "An Archaeological Study of Clay Pipes from the King's Bastion, Fortress of Louisbourg," Canadian Historic Sites: Occasional Papers in Archaeology and History, No. 2 [1971], pp. 55-122, Ottawa.)

Walker, Kent G., and Stephen L. Cumbaa
"Life on the Frontier, 1665-1760: A Zooarchaeological Look at Fort Chambly, Quebec." Manuscript on file, Zooarchaeological Identification Centre, National Museum of Natural Sciences, Ottawa, 1982.

PROVENANCE AND NEGATIVE NUMBERS
OF ILLUSTRATED OBJECTS

Fig.	Artifact	Negative	Fig.	Artifact	Negative
2	16G8A32-2Q	16G-118/ACM/PR-6/P-11	26	16G4U9-1Q	16G-118/ACM/PR-6/P-21
3	16G8A32-4Q	16G-118/ACM/PR-6/P-56	27	16G8A62-3Q	16G-118/ACM/PR-6/P-27
4	16G8A32-31Q	16G-118/ACM/PR-6/67-1	28	16G8A32-25Q	16G-118/ACM/PR-6/P-51
5	16G8A64-3Q	16G-118/ACM/PR-6/P-63	29	16G8K28-5Q	16G-118/ACM/PR-6/P-66
6	16G8A50-1Q	16G-118/ACM/PR-6/P-52	30	16G4J12-1Q	16G-118/ACM/PR-6/P-58
7	16G8A36-14Q	16G-118/ACM/PR-6/P-62	31	16G8K28-3Q	16G-118/ACM/PR-6/P-50
8	16G8K12-1Q	16G-118/ACM/PR-6/27-5	32	16G5G14-1Q	16G-118/ACM/PR-6/P-65
9 a	16G8A32-30Q		33	16G5A7-1Q	16G-118/ACM/PR-6/P-23
b	16G8A32-16Q		34	16G5G5-1Q	16G-118/ACM/PR-6/P-28
c	16G8A32-8Q		35	16G4D9-1Q	16G-118/ACM/PR-6/P-69
d	16G8A32-37Q		36	16G8K25-4Q	16G-118/ACM/PR-6/P-33
e	16G8A32-38Q	16G-118/ACM/PR-6/P-15	37	16G8K1-1Q	16G-118/ACM/PR-6/74-1
f	16G8A32-40Q		38	16G4J11-4Q	16G-118/ACM/PR-6/P-35
g	16G8A32-41Q		39	16G4T7-1Q	16G-118/ACM/PR-6/P-59
h	16G8A32-23Q		40	16G8A50-9Q	16G-118/ACM/PR-6/P-43
10	16G8A36-13Q	16G-118/ACM/PR-6/P-24	41	16G8A50-10Q	16G-118/ACM/PR-6/P-60
11	16G8A32-27Q	16G-118/ACM/PR-6/65-4	42	16G5G4-9Q	16G-118/ACM/PR-6/P-26
12	16G8A32-28Q	16G-118/ACM/PR-6/63-12	43	16G8A65-1Q	16G-118/ACM/PR-6/P-1
13	16G8A32-14Q	16G-118/ACM/PR-6/P-12	44	16G4T3-2Q	16G-118/ACM/PR-6/P-57
14	16G8A36-15Q	16G-118/ACM/PR-6/P-31	45	16G8P5-1Q	16G-118/ACM/PR-6/P-38
15	16G4G8-1Q	16G-118/ACM/PR-6/P-25	46	16G5G18-5Q	16G-118/ACM/PR-6/P-55
16	16G8A36-11Q	16G-118/ACM/PR-6/71-11	47	16G5G9-5Q	16G-118/ACM/PR-6/P-61
17	16G8A32-39Q	16G-118/ACM/PR-6/P-41	48	16G4F6-2Q	16G-118/ACM/PR-6/P-47
18	16G8A32-36Q		49	16G4T4-1Q	16G-118/ACM/PR-6/P-44
19	16G8A32-21Q	16G-118/ACM/PR-6/P-17	50	16G5G17-1Q	16G-118/ACM/PR-6/64-2
20	16G8A32-10Q	16G-118/ACM/PR-6/60-11	51	16G8P6-2Q	16G-118/ACM/PR-6/P-49
21	16G8A32-33Q	16G-118/ACM/PR-6/P-40	52	16G8P6-5Q	16G-118/ACM/PR-6/P-29
22	16G8A32-34Q	16G-118/ACM/PR-6/87-4	53	16G8K2-2Q	16G-118/ACM/PR-6/P-48
23	16G8A32-24Q	16G-118/ACM/PR-6/P-39	54	16G9W17-1Q	16G-118/ACM/PR-6/P-20
24	16G8A62-1Q	16G-118/ACM/PR-6/P-46	55	16G9Y4-1Q	16G-118/ACM/PR-6/P-18
25	16G8K18-1Q	16G-118/ACM/PR-6/P-42	56	16G9Y4-2Q	16G-118/ACM/PR-6/P-19